Rational Risk Policy

ARNE RYDE
8 December 1944–1 April 1968

Rational Risk Policy

The 1996 Arne Ryde Memorial Lectures

W. Kip Viscusi

CLARENDON PRESS · OXFORD
1998

Oxford University Press, Great Clarendon Street, Oxford OX2 6DP

Oxford New York

Athens Auckland Bangkok Bogota Bombay
Buenos Aires Calcutta Cape Town Dar es Salaam
Delhi Florence Hong Kong Istanbul Karachi
Kuala Lumpur Madras Madrid Melbourne
Mexico City Nairobi Paris Singapore
Taipei Tokyo Toronto Warsaw

and associated companies in
Berlin Ibadan

Oxford is a trade mark of Oxford University Press

Published in the United States
by Oxford University Press Inc., New York

British Library Cataloguing in Publication Data
Data available

Library of Congress Cataloging in Publication Data
Data available
ISBN 0–19–829363–1 (hbk)

1 3 5 7 9 10 8 6 4 2

Typeset by Hope Services (Abingdon) Ltd.
Printed in Great Britain
on acid-free paper by
Biddles Ltd.
Guildford & King's Lynn

The Arne Ryde Foundation

ARNE RYDE was an exceptionally promising young student on the
doctorate programme at the Department of Economics at the
University of Lund. He died after an automobile accident in 1968
when only twenty-three years old. In his memory his parents Valborg
Ryde and pharmacist Sven Ryde established the Arne Ryde
Foundation for the advancement of research at our department. We
are most grateful to them. The Foundation has made possible important activities which our ordinary resources could not have afforded.

In agreement with Valborg and Sven Ryde, we have decided to use
the funds made available by the Foundation to finance major initia-
tives. Since 1973 we have arranged a series of symposia in various
fields of theoretical and applied economics. In 1990 we published
'Seven Schools of Macroeconomic Thought' by Edmund S. Phelps,
the first issue in a series of Arne Ryde Memorial Lectures. Thomas J.
Sargent's 'Bounded Rationality in Macroeconomics' followed in
1993, and 'High Inflation' by Professors Daniel Heymann and Axel
Leijonhufvud in 1995. The present book by Professor W. Kip
Viscusi, based on lectures held at Lund University in May 1996, is
the fourth issue in this series. We are very glad and grateful that
Professor Viscusi agreed to come to Lund to give his Arne Ryde
Memorial Lectures.

Bjørn Thalberg

Preface

THIS book is the written version of the Arne Ryde Memorial Lectures that I delivered at Lund University in Sweden on May 20–21, 1996. The topic of these lectures seems to be particularly appropriate for this lecture series. Arne Ryde was killed in an automobile accident, which led to the endowment of this lecture series.

These lectures will address a variety of issues pertinent to this tragic event. How should society think about the prevention of accidents such as the one that killed Arne Ryde? Is there a sensible way to approach transportation safety decisions in economic terms? To what extent do government regulatory agencies make sound decisions to protect our welfare? Are resources to protect us from various risks being allocated sensibly? Are regulatory decisions rational or are they contaminated by the same types of biases that may plague individual risk-taking decisions?

As this volume will document, the answers to these questions indicate that there is considerable potential to make regulations less costly and more protective. Even after decades of experience with transportation safety regulation, this risk area still does not receive sufficient regulatory protection relative to other risks. Dimly understood risks with remote possibilities of occurrence command more of our attention than the truly fundamental risks to our lives. The guidelines that I present for regulatory policy in these lectures provide an economic framework for designing more efficient and more protective safety policies.

The format for the lectures was a series of six lectures of approximately one to one-and-a-half hours each over a two-day period. The intent of the book is to preserve the accessibility of the lectures, while at the same time providing a comprehensive overview of economic principles for sound risk regulation. The audience for the lectures consisted of graduate students and faculty at Lund University as well as other Scandinavian institutions. I would particularly like to thank Professor Bjørn Thalberg of the Economics Department at Lund University for inviting me to participate in what he has made a very distinguished lecture series. Professor Göran Skogh of the Department of Economics and Institute of Industrial Environmental Studies served as the principal organizer and a superb host for the lectures. I would also like to thank many other participating faculties for their comments, especially Professor Alf Risa, of the University of Bergen, Norway.

The usual economic prescription for regulatory policy involves advocating basic efficiency principles, such as ensuring that the benefits of these efforts are commensurate with the costs. The organizing principle of these lectures goes beyond this notion. These lectures explore the theme that the irrationality of individual decisions is often embodied in government regulation. Citizen pressures often generate the impetus for risk regulation. The task of the government should be to address these inadequacies in individual behavior. However, since government regulation responds to political pressures, including those generated by misperceptions, the role of the government is often to institutionalize these inadequacies rather than to overcome them. In addition, government officials may be subject to the same human failings that consumers and workers exhibit in their private decisions, leading to potential distortions in government policy. This book will detail these shortcomings as well as identify appropriate targets for improved regulatory performance.

Although much of the empirical evidence draws on the US experience, for which there is a very extensive regulatory structure that has been in place for a long period of time, the principles involved here are truly international in character. Participating countries in the OECD activities, for example, have espoused broad principles for regulatory reform not unlike some of the efficiency guidelines generally advocated by economists.

The organization of the book directly parallels that of the lectures, with two exceptions. The introductory chapter and Chapter 2 comprised the first lecture, and Chapter 7 and the concluding Chapter 8 comprised the last lecture of the series.

In addition to receiving financial support from Arne Ryde Foundation, I also would like to acknowledge additional support that fostered the writing of this book. The Sheldon Seevak Research Fund, the Harvard Law School Faculty Research Fund, and Harvard's Olin Center for Law and Economics provided partial support. I would also like to thank Tracy Kuczak, my former editorial assistant, who played a key role in facilitating the research and writing of this book. Michael Jones-Lee, Paul Anand, Thomas Kniesner, and an anonymous reviewer provided excellent comments.

W.K.V.

12 June 1997

Contents

Figures

Tables

1
Introduction

Policies addressed at reducing risk and compensating risk victims have become increasingly prominent components of the role of government in modern society. The costs of risk and environmental regulations mandated by the government are considerable, and the increasing role of liability for risk threatens to transform the functioning of the insurance industry throughout the world.

The basic facts of regulatory activity are quite impressive. In the United States, the annual costs of risk and environmental regulation now exceed $150 billion annually.[1] Indeed, these costs of risk and environmental regulations now total twice the value of the costs of all traditional economic regulations such as those pertaining to prices and antitrust policy. This dominance of the role of risk and environmental regulation is likely to become increasingly stark. Environmental regulations are the fastest growing component of regulatory costs, and the increased deregulation of matters such as airplane fares and trucking rates has substantially reduced the costs associated with these regulatory efforts.

Liability costs are also on the rise. The costs of workers' compensation for job accidents in the United States now equal the costs of unemployment compensation—a social insurance policy that has long been prominent in the labor economics literature. The additional role of tort liability for risky products and jobs has transformed the role of liability in modern society. Major corporations now declare bankruptcy in the presence of these costs, and even the most venerable insurance institution, Lloyd's of London, tottered on the brink of insolvency and was recently restructured.[2] These

[1] See Hopkins (1992) for fuller documentation of these costs. These estimates are reprinted and discussed on pp. 33–4 of Viscusi, Vernon, and Harrington (1995). An earlier annual tally of costs with more agency detail appears in Viscusi (1983). Adams (1995) provides an excellent risk policy perspective on the UK.

[2] For an account of the resolution of the crisis at Lloyd's, see 'The Temple of Good Fortune', *The Economist*, Aug. 31, 1996, pp. 59–60.

difficulties arise because hazards such as asbestos and major oil spills are not small independent risks but multi-billion-dollar losses.

The ever-increasing liability cost levels in no way imply that there is not a constructive role for risk regulation and liability policies. Situations involving individual risk decisions and environmental consequences are prominent potential targets of government intervention. Decisions involving risk often pose substantial difficulties for personal decisions. The well known problems associated with environmental externalities provide additional impetus for government intervention. The primary question for policy is: how can we target the regulatory expenditures to best promote society's interests? These lectures will be concerned with the foundations of government policy, many of which are specifically linked to individual rationality. While government policy could ameliorate these shortcomings, in many instances the effect of government policy is to mirror the types of irrationality that are reflected in individual decisions.

In these lectures I will begin by addressing the shortcomings in individual behavior in Chapter 2, which focuses on how people form risk beliefs and make choices under uncertainty. To the extent that these decisions are flawed because people do not have a sound understanding of the risks they face, there will be a potential role for government provision of risk information. This topic is the focus of Chapter 3, which explores the role of hazard warnings and other related information transfer efforts.

Since a zero level of risk is infeasible, ultimately we must make some tradeoffs between the risks we face and other competing objectives. The most widely used metric for measuring these tradeoffs is the risk–money tradeoff, or the value of a statistical life. Chapter 4 presents evidence on these values and considers how they might be used in a policy context. The first task of regulatory policy is to ensure that risks are reduced, not increased. Chapter 5 explores the increasingly prominent methodology of risk–risk analysis, which explores the diverse effects of regulation, some of which may be counterproductive. Chapter 6 examines current practices of risk analysis and regulatory policy approaches. A disturbing pattern of these efforts is that they often embody irrational responses to risk rather than fostering the kinds of policy that would allocate our safety expenditures to generate the greatest improvement in individual welfare. Chapter 7 examines the increasingly prominent role of

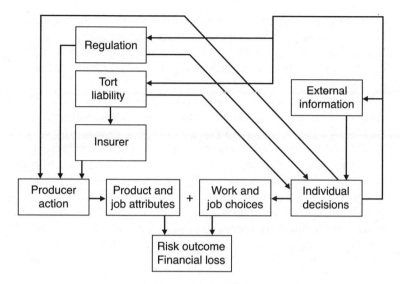

FIG. 1.1 The Accident Generating Process

liability and social insurance, and Chapter 8 outlines an agenda for regulatory reform.

Figure 1.1 sketches the linkage between these various factors that drive risk and environmental outcomes. Consumers generally make decisions on a decentralized basis with respect to risky products and activities. External information provided as a result of regulatory efforts is part of this information context, as are the incentives generated through insurance company efforts, e.g. higher insurance rates for motorists with violations for driving while intoxicated. Decisions by producers are subject not only to the usual market influences of the preferences of workers and consumers, but also to the role of regulation, tort liability, and insurers—all of which influence these risk decisions.

The multiplicity of the institutional linkages in Figure 1.1 is a mixed blessing. Multiple societal institutions increase the variety of policy mechanisms that we can exploit to influence many policy concerns, ranging from an improved informational basis for decisions to compensation of accident victims. The diversity of institutions also creates the potential for innovation and comprehensive policies that fill the gaps in the policy structure that might be left by the failure of other institutional mechanisms to address the policy concerns. However, there is a potential danger in the multiplicity of institutions in that these efforts may be duplicative, not reinforcing. The combined influence of these efforts also may create unintended consequences.

In the standard market paradigm of economists, the decentralized decisions by individuals lead to optimal societal outcomes in a wide variety of situations. This fortuitous result does not generalize to decentralized actions by a variety of government actors. These efforts frequently lead to duplicative incentives and policy overlaps that are not socially desirable. By considering the diverse social mechanisms that work and their interaction, we will be better able to exploit the comparative advantage of the different societal institutions and to eliminate the inefficiencies that arise from competing efforts.

2

Risk Beliefs and Individual Rationality

Individual risk perceptions are often in error. However, it is an over-simplification simply to note that people make mistakes with respect to how they perceive risk and behave in the presence of uncertainty. Many of these biases are systematic and will have an influence on the character of individual decisions and the rationale for government intervention.

One of the most prominent biases pertains to the risk level. Figure 2.1 sketches individual assessments of the mortality risk from different outcomes on the vertical axis as a function of the actual number

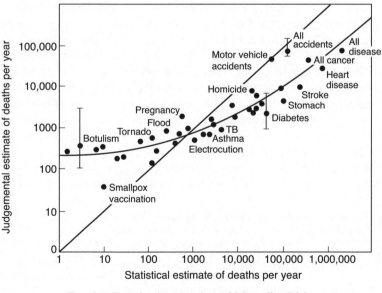

FIG. 2.1 Perceived versus Actual Mortality Risks
Source: Fischoff *et al.* (1961), p. 29.

of deaths from these different causes on the horizontal axis. If perceived risks equal the actual risks, the perceptions would lie along the 45-degree line. The actual pattern is that individuals overestimate the small risks they face, such as those posed by botulism, tornadoes, and floods. In contrast, they underestimate the more substantial risks, such as those from stroke, heart disease, and cancer.[1]

THE PROSPECTIVE REFERENCE THEORY MODEL

This phenomenon, as well as related aspects of choice under uncertainty, led me to formulate a model that I termed 'prospective reference theory.' When considering uncertain prospects, individuals bring to bear reference points for thinking about the risk. These reference points simply represent a formal recognition that prior beliefs influence risk perceptions, even for abstract experimental lotteries. Given these reference points, individuals act in a rational Bayesian manner. However, they are not fully informed, and they may start with prior probabilistic beliefs that are in error. The basics of the approach are quite simple and follow the formulation that one would adopt using a standard Bayesian learning model in which individual priors are characterized by a beta distribution of priors.[2] In forming their prior beliefs, individuals have an assumed prior assessment q_i of risk outcome i and an associated precision γ. In effect, people act as if they have drawn γ balls from a Bernoulli urn, of which a fraction q_i outcomes are associated with outcome i. The individual then acquires additional information, which implies a risk p_i of outcome i. The parameter ξ represents the informational content associated with this new information. In effect, this new information has the same informational content as drawing ξ balls from an urn. In the case of a classroom experiment involving risk, which is the foundation of much of the work on choice under uncertainty, p_i would be

---

[1] Using the data developed by the psychologists whose work gave rise to Figure 2.1 (see Lichtenstein *et al.* 1978), I have estimated the relationship between perceived and actual risk for their sample (see Viscusi 1992*a*). One cannot reject the hypothesis that there is a linear relationship following the Bayesian learning model that I will sketch below. A recent overview of the work on risk by psychologists appears in Yates (1992).

[2] A similar formulation results from using a normal distribution assumption, but the beta distribution is much more flexible and can generate a wide variety of skewed and symmetric shapes. Other reference points for judging rationality are discussed in Anand (1991).

the stated probability given to respondents as part of the study and ξ, the subjective informational weight that individuals attach to the experimental information. The usual assumption concerning risk experiments in the literature is that the experimental risk information is all that matters, or $\xi \rightarrow \infty$. The total information content for both the prior beliefs and the information is $\gamma + \xi$; i.e., the total information available is equivalent to $\gamma + \xi$ draws from a Bernoulli urn.[3]

An individual's posterior assessment of $P(p_i)$ for outcome i with stated probability p_i simply equals a weighted average of the prior risk belief plus the probability conveyed by the new risk information. The weights applied to each of these terms equal the fraction of the informational content associated with them. More specifically, we can characterize individuals' posterior beliefs $P(p_i)$ as a linear weighted average of the prior and new risk information, or

$$P(p_i) = \frac{\gamma q_i + \xi p_i}{\gamma + \xi}. \tag{2.1}$$

In the case in which the individual is dealing with an abstract lottery or has no detailed prior risk information, researchers generally ignore the role of prior beliefs. However, in my formulation the assumption of the model is that all n possible states are equally likely, so that the value of q_i is $1/n$. To operationalize the posterior belief equation (2.1), one simply substitutes $1/n$ for q_i. Thus, in this formulation the posterior probability that is the effective perceived probability that is pertinent in thinking about abstract experiments is given by

$$P(p_i) = \frac{\gamma(1/n) + \xi p_i}{\gamma + \xi}. \tag{2.2}$$

The two main amendments to this formulation are that individuals perceive certain events of 0 and 1 accurately, or

$$P(0) = 0 \quad \text{and} \quad P(1) = 1. \tag{2.3}$$

The graphical implications of this framework appear in Figure 2.2. The perceived probability is a simple linear function of the stated probability. At the probability p_f, the perceived and stated probabilities are equal. Below this value individuals overestimate the risk, and above this value they underestimate it. Whenever the prior risk

---

[3] The value of $\gamma + \xi$ constitutes the denominator in the expression on the right of equation (2.1).

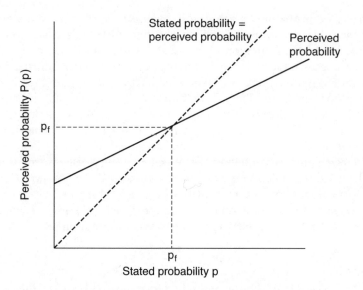

FIG. 2.2 Relation between Perceived and Stated Probabilities

assessment q_i exceeds the stated probability p_i, the perceived probability lies above the stated probability. Similarly, the region of underestimation in Figure 2.2 arises when q_i is below p_i.

What is striking about this framework of equations (2.1)–(2.3) is that the theory predicts that the observed pattern of overestimating small risks and underestimating large risks will always occur. It is not simply an outcome that could occur given some arbitrary specification of risk beliefs that is specific to a particular context. Moreover, this model has as its grounding a rational Bayesian learning model, with the primary distinguishing feature that individuals are not perfectly informed but instead are acting in a world in which the information they have received is not fully informative. They simply do not take the information presented to them at face value, and if they do, the full information model emerges as a special case.

The shape of the perceived probability function in Figure 2.2 also indicates the perceptional basis for people's willingness to pay a certainty premium for a reduction in risk to zero. As the evidence that we will consider below indicates, people are willing to pay an additional premium for the assurance that there is zero risk. This certainty premium goes beyond the estimated risk–money tradeoff values. Perhaps for that reason, government food safety officials, for example, declare that governmental food inspections have made our food 'safe' rather than saying that the number of food poisoning deaths this year will be reasonably small.

The practical importance of the biases in risk beliefs will depend on the risk contexts. For abstract lotteries, prior reference point effects may play a substantial role since the hypothetical lottery may not be credible. For real-world lotteries for which there is substantial information about the risk, the ratio ξ/γ may be substantial, as actual risk lottery experience may dominate. Workers on jobs involving acute accident risks often have very accurate risk perceptions since they can draw on a variety of information sources including their own experiences and observations of a variety of workplace characteristics correlated with riskiness.

This prospective reference theory model predicts several major anomalies in the literature, including effects of the representativeness heuristic (i.e. the dampening of the influence of the differences in base rate characteristics given to respondents) and the isolation effect (i.e. reversal of attitudes toward lotteries within compound lotteries when the lotteries are decomposed). More generally, this model yields as a *theorem* what Kahneman and Tversky observed as an empirical regularity, which they refer to as the 'general principle underlying violations of the substitution axiom' in choice under uncertainty. Kahneman and Tversky (1979) include this hypothesized relationship as the key perceptional *assumption* in their prospect theory model.[4] The essence of this principle is that, as any probabilities p and q $(p < q)$ are multiplied by some scale factor a

---

[4] In our notation, suppose that probabilities p and q are increased by some scale factor a.

$$\frac{\partial}{\partial a} \frac{P(ap)}{P(aq)} = \frac{\gamma\xi(1/n)\,(p-q)}{[\gamma(1/n) + \xi qa]^2}.$$

For the special case where $p < q$ and $a < 1$, we get the result

$$\frac{P(p)}{P(q)} \leq \frac{P(ap)}{P(aq)}.$$

This inequality is a necessary *prediction* of the prospective reference theory, whereas it is identified *ex post* as an 'empirical regularity' and an assumption in Kahneman and Tversky's (1979) prospect theory model.

(where $a < 1$), then their ratio appears to be larger. Shrinking the magnitude of probabilities proportionally makes them look more similar, so that (0.0001/0.0002) appears larger and closer to 1 than (0.1/0.2).

It is instructive to apply the prospective reference theory approach to the well known Allais paradox, since this is perhaps the most prominent violation of the expected utility model. In the standard version of the Allais paradox, individuals prefer the certain lottery (1, 100) in which they have a probability of one of receiving a payoff of 100 to the uncertain lottery (0.1, 500; 0.89, 100; 0.01, 0). In terms of our perceptional notation,

$$P(1)U(100) > P(0.10)U(500) + P(0.89)U(100) + P(0.01)U(0).$$
(2.4)

The contradiction in behavior arises once preferences are reversed upon subtracting the 0.89 probability of winning a payoff 100 from both sides of the equation; i.e., the lottery (0.11, 100; 0.89, 0) is not as attractive as (0.10, 500; 0.90, 0). Based on the prospective reference theory notation, this pattern of preferences is that

$$P(0.11)\ U(100) + P(0.89)\ U(0) < P(0.10)\ U(500) + P(0.90)\ U(0).$$
(2.5)

This pair of inequalities is inconsistent in the standard expected utility model for which $P(p) = p$. A particularly striking implication of prospective reference theory is that, not only is this pair of inequalities not contradictory, but a potential reversal in preferences is always consistent with the model. The only exception is the limiting case in which the probabilistic information provided is treated as being fully informative (i.e., ξ is infinite).

To substitute the prospective reference theory values for the perceptions for the values of $P(p)$ in equations (2.4) and (2.5), note that the value of $1/n$ differs for the different lotteries since n is the number of lottery outcomes. The value of n is 1 for the first lottery in (2.4), 3 for the second lottery in (2.4), 2 for the first lottery of (2.5), and 2 for the second lottery in (2.5). Making the substitution, (2.4) becomes

$$U(100) > \frac{0.33\gamma + 0.1\xi}{\gamma + \xi}\ U(500) + \frac{0.33\gamma + 0.89\xi}{\gamma + \xi}\ U(100) + \frac{0.33\gamma + 0.01\xi}{\gamma + \xi},$$
(2.6)

and (2.5) becomes

$$\frac{0.5\gamma + 0.11\xi}{\gamma + \xi} \, U(100) + \frac{0.5\gamma + 0.89\xi}{\gamma + \xi} \, U(0) < \frac{0.5\gamma + 0.1\xi}{\gamma + \xi} \, U(500)$$

$$+ \frac{0.5\gamma + 0.9\xi}{\gamma + \xi} \, U(0). \tag{2.7}$$

With no loss of generality, set $U(0)$ equal to 0 so that (2.6) simplifies to

$$U(100) > \frac{0.33\gamma + 0.1\xi}{0.67\gamma + 0.11\xi} \, U(500), \tag{2.8}$$

and (2.7) simplifies to

$$U(100) < \frac{0.5\gamma + 0.1\xi}{0.5\gamma + 0.11\xi} \, U(500). \tag{2.9}$$

Excluding the limiting full information in which $\xi \to a$,

$$\frac{0.5\gamma + 0.1\xi}{0.5\gamma + 0.11\xi} > \frac{0.33\gamma + 0.1\xi}{0.67\gamma + 0.11\xi}, \tag{2.10}$$

which always holds.

The role of the perceptional biases incorporated in prospective reference theory consequently creates the impetus for the kind of phenomenon underlying the Allais paradox. It is useful to recall equations (2.4) and (2.5) to examine why this occurs. People treat the perceived probability of a payoff of 100 in (2.4) at face value. However, this certainty effect alone does not account for all such phenomena. The role of the prior assessed probability for each outcome that equals 1/2 for the lottery on the right hand side of (2.5) enhances the attractiveness of this lottery with a payoff of 500. Although there is a role for prior probabilities for the analogous lottery on the right side of (2.4), the reference probability of $1/n$ is 1/3 for this three-possible-outcome case so that the weight on the payoff of 500 is not as great as it is in (2.5).

IMPLICATIONS FOR SAFETY BEHAVIOR: THE PRECAUTIONARY BEHAVIOR PARADOX

The structure of risk perceptions embodied in the prospective reference theory model also has major implications for the rationality of

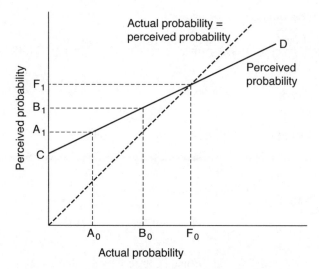

FIG. 2.3 Relation between Actual and Perceived Probabilities

risk-taking decisions. Figure 2.3 presents the graphical basis for the analysis.[5] Individuals have a perceived risk perception function *CD* for which they overestimate all probabilities below F_0.

Consider first the effect on compensating differentials for job risks or the risk premium reductions individuals must receive to be willing to purchase hazardous products. For actual risk probabilities in $(0, F_0)$ people overestimate risks, and individuals underassess risks above F_0. Since most risks from products and jobs tend to be relatively small, this influence will tend to lead to excessive risk assessments and market overreactions to risk.

How such risk biases affect risk levels selected and protective behavior is, however, a more complicated, and possibly counterintuitive, phenomenon. It is possible to distinguish several predicted effects of this perceptional structure, not all of which are in the expected direction. First, clearly, the total risk compensation that people will require, either in terms of higher wages for risky jobs or lower prices for risky products, will be greater if they overassess the magnitude of the risk. The level of the perceived risk drives these decisions, and the biases discussed above influence these perceptions.

[5] The formalization of this model appears in Viscusi (1990*b*).

Second, the risk premium in terms of the additional compensation required for any given loss will rise as the size of the loss increases. Upward biases in the level of risk beliefs increase the expected value of losses, where this premium due to misperception increases with the size of the loss. Such money–loss tradeoffs will also increase with the extent of risk overestimation. Third, people will tend to overinsure if they exaggerate the magnitude of the risk, and to underinsure otherwise. These factors will tend to make market responses to small risks too great, leading to suboptimal risk levels and excessive insurance of small risks. In contrast, large underestimated risks will be too great and will be underinsured.

These effects follow the expected pattern, but there is a fourth predicted effect that is more surprising. In particular, the perceptional biases that lead to risk overestimation will also generate inadequate incentives for risk precautions. The starting point for understanding this result is to note that the level of safety precautions that will be selected is not driven by the level of the probability but rather by how this probability changes with precautionary actions. Marginal effects rather than levels are the matter of concern. The risk perception function flattens the responsiveness of perceived probabilities to changes in actual probabilities, making them seem smaller than they are. The incentive for safety precautions will be less than in the accurate perceptions case since the perceived safety improvement will be less than the actual risk reduction.

Consider a simple model in which the assessed risk of accident $P(p)$ depends on the prior assessed reference risk level q and the risk p associated with the particular activity.[6] The value of p in turn depends on the level of precautionary investment c, where $dp/dc < 0$. The risk perceived P of an accident is consequently

$$P = \frac{\gamma q + \xi p(c)}{\gamma + \xi}. \tag{2.11}$$

The choice problem is to maximize expected utility, where U is the utility function for good health, V is the utility function after an injury, and I is income, or

$$\underset{c}{\text{Max }} Z = \left(1 - \frac{\gamma q + \xi p(c)}{\gamma + \xi}\right) U(I-c) + \frac{\gamma q + \xi p(c)}{\gamma + \xi} V(I-c). \tag{2.12}$$

---

[6] The variant of the model including insurance choices as well appears in Viscusi (1990*b*).

The optimal precaution sets

$$\frac{-dp}{dc} = \frac{\gamma + \xi}{\xi} \frac{(1-P)\ U' + PV'}{U-V}. \qquad (2.13)$$

In the presence of optimal insurance, $U' = V'$, so that this requirement simplifies to

$$\frac{-dp}{dc} = \frac{\gamma + \xi}{\xi} \frac{U'}{U-V}. \qquad (2.14)$$

The negative of the marginal effect of precautionary investments on the risk p equals the positive term on the right side of (2.14). However, since $(\gamma + \xi)/\xi$ exceeds 1, the net effect of the role of imperfect information is to impose a more demanding test on the efficacy of precautions and to discourage precautionary behavior.

In terms of Figure 2.3, consider a safety precaution, such as wearing seatbelts or protective equipment. Protective behavior will diminish the risk level from B_0 to A_0. However, the risk change perceived by the individual is only B_1 to A_1. This perceived risk decrease will necessarily be less than the actual decline since all perceived probability functions CD are flatter than the 45-degree line.

This perceptional effect leads to what one might view as a paradoxical result. Consider a situation involving small risks. People will overestimate the risk, require excessive compensation to face the risk, and overinsure against it. These are all risk-reducing types of behavior. However, they will also be excessively complacent about taking protective actions to diminish the risk. Actions to alter the risk through protective behavior will be suboptimal. Perhaps somewhat paradoxically, the precautionary response to risks is excessive intransigence and paralysis in the face of exaggerated small hazards that people otherwise try to avoid. We will term this effect the 'precautionary behavior paradox.'

EMPIRICAL CONSEQUENCES OF PERCEPTIONAL BIASES

Consumer willingness to pay for decreases in risk for household chemical products embodies the types of biases reflected in the prospective reference theory formulation. Table 2.1 summarizes consumer willingness to pay for successive reductions in risk for two dif-

TABLE 2.1.   Marginal Valuations of Reducing Both Risks by 5/10,000

Starting risk injuries/ 10,000 bottles	Incremental willingness to pay ($ bottle)			
	Insecticide		Toilet bowl cleaner	
	Inhalation— skin poisoning	Inhalation— child poisoning	Gassing— eyeburn	Gassing— child poisoning
15	1.04	1.84	0.65	0.99
10	0.34	0.54	0.19	0.24
5	2.41	5.71	0.83	0.99

ferent hypothetical products. The first two columns pertain to pairs of risk associated with insecticide, where they survey presented the inhalation–skin poisoning risk pair to respondents without children and the inhalation–child poisoning pair to respondents with children. The final two columns of the table pertain to risk pairs for toilet bowl cleaner, where the gassing–eyeburn risk pair was for households without children and the gassing–child poisoning risk pair was for the households with young children.

From the standpoint of economic theory, individuals should be willing to pay successively smaller amounts for each incremental risk reduction. The starting risk was 15/10,000 for each component of the risk pair. The first row of statistics in Table 2.1 is the respondents' average willingness to pay per bottle for a reformulated version of the product that decreased the risk by 5/10,000. These values range from $0.65 to $1.84. The second row of statistics in the table is their willingness to pay for the next incremental risk reduction starting at 10/10,000 and decreasing it to 5/10,000. This amount reflects a diminishing willingness to pay, which was consistent with theoretical predictions. Somewhat surprisingly, respondents are willing to pay the greatest amount for a risk reduction for the last incremental risk decrement from 5/10,000 to zero. This amount dwarfs the previous willingness to pay from 10/10,000 to 5/10,000 in every case. Moreover, for both pairs of insecticide risks, respondents' willingness to pay for the last incremental risk reduction 5/10,000 exceeds their combined willingness to pay for the two previous risk reductions, which were twice as great in terms of the risk decrease.

This pattern reflects the influence of certainty premiums.

Respondents' overassessment of low-probability events, as compared with the zero risk alternative—possibly in conjunction with any economic value that zero risk offers in terms of additional peace of mind—accounts for the strong preference for the certainty of zero risk.

This preference is often embodied in government policies as well. In the United States, food additive regulations under the Delaney Clause specifically exclude from food all chemical additives that are found to pose any nonzero risk of carcinogenicity. This phenomenon generates severe distortions in the character of chemical regulations, which we will explore in Chapter 6.

An even starker phenomenon is the asymmetry in respondents' attitude to increases in risk. What if the product risk increases by some small increment rather than decreases? Table 2.2 summarizes for each of the risk pairs the attitudes toward a 1/10,000 risk increase from a baseline risk value of 15/10,000. Respondents' attitudes toward a 5/10,000 risk increase, which would have provided comparability with Table 2.1, were so extreme that it would have threatened the viability of the entire survey. Even with a risk increase of only 1/10,000, the majority of the respondents said they would refuse to purchase the product at any price, even if they were given the product for free and offered a subsidy. As the results in Table 2.2 indicate, for the different products from 62 to 77 percent would not purchase the riskier formulation at any price. This result occurred even after the respondents were offered the product without cost and were given the option of being paid to use the product. Moreover, the small minority of consumers who were willing to buy it required a

TABLE 2.2.   Responses to Risk Increase (+1, +1) Valuation Questions[a]

Injury pair	% for whom product is too risky to purchase	Mean value ($/bottle) of positive responses
Inhalation—skin poisoning	77.2	2.86
Inhalation—child poisoning	68.1	3.19
Eyeburns—gassing	61.5	5.52
Gassing—child poisoning	74.3	1.28

[a] This question asked subjects what price discount they would require on the new product to accept an additional risk of 1/10,000 for both injuries, starting with risks of 15 injuries per 10,000 bottles sold for both injuries.

much greater price reduction for a 1/10,000 risk increase than they were willing to pay for 10/10,000 risk decrease. The extreme case is for the sample considering the eyeburn-gassing risk pair for toilet bowl cleaner who were willing to pay $0.65 to reduce the risk from 15/10,000 to 10/10,000, but who wanted a price cut of $5.52 to incur a risk increase of only 1/10,000.

This phenomenon gives rise to what my colleagues and I have termed a 'reference risk effect.'[7] Disturbances in the accustomed risk level may generate exaggerated responses to risk. Subsequent studies have generated related evidence of starting-point biases and status quo effects. These extreme responses are not predicted by prospective reference theory or other models, though the role of such effects can be incorporated as an explicit amendment to such models.

This phenomenon will create excessive reactions to newly discovered risks, such as recently identified carcinogens. There will consequently be more public impetus for regulation of products, and related novel risks. The market will give excessive rewards to firms that eliminate small risks, as in the case when Perrier recalled its bottled water after the presence of negligible concentrations of benzene was publicized. Errors of commission that create new risks, such as approval of a risky new pharmaceutical product, will likewise generate extreme risk reactions. In contrast, there will be comparative inattention to more accustomed risks that we face, such as those posed by our diet and lack of exercise.

RISK AMBIGUITY EFFECTS

Not all risks are known with precision. The most highly publicized risk of 1996 was Mad Cow Disease. One widely cited British scientist's estimate was that the risk of Creutzfeldt–Jakob disease (CJD) from British cattle would lead to 500–500,000 British deaths.[8] Put somewhat differently, the risk could be fairly small or catastrophic.

---

[7] See Viscusi, Magat, and Huber (1987).
[8] See 'Mad Cows and Englishmen,' *The Economist* (March 30, 1996), p. 25. Mad Cow Disease is the infectious disease in animals known as bovine spongiform encephalopathy or BSE. The human form is a variant of Creutzfeldt–Jakob disease. A series of 12 British deaths from CJD in early 1996 led to the concern with Mad Cow Disease. An excellent assessment of some pertinent economic issues appears in Anand and Forshner (1995).

The public's response in Britain developed into a major health crisis after 16 people under the age of 40 developed CJD. The British government enacted stringent measures in response to the CJD deaths. There was, however, no evidence that these ailments were linked to beef consumption, though the effect of CJD on humans is similar to the effect of Mad Cow Disease on cows. The absence of firm evidence does not, however, mean that the cattle are risk-free, only that our knowledge of the risks is imprecise. The subsequent slaughter of cattle and other disruptive effects of Mad Cow Disease led to economic losses worldwide estimated to be as high as $10 billion. Whether such costs are a sensible price to pay depends on the magnitude of the risk, the exact extent of which is still not known.

How do people respond to ambiguity in risk possibilities such as this? The presence of risk ambiguity can generate irrational responses to risk. In the classic Ellsberg paradox, the task of the respondent is to win a prize by naming the correct color of a ball drawn from an urn.[9] Urn 1 contains 50 red balls and 50 black balls. Urn 2 contains 100 red and black balls, but the mixture is unspecified. Which urn will the respondent pick?

In general, respondents prefer urn 1, which offers a precise probability of success. This distinct preference is somewhat anomalous, since the urns are in fact equivalent if there is no opportunity for learning in a multi-period trial situation. For example, one can produce a 'hard' probability of success with urn 2 by flipping a fair coin to decide on the chosen ball color. If one believes that the mixture in urn 2 is slanted in a particular direction, one can always have better than a 0.5 probability of success. People tend to prefer the precise chance of success and to avoid the ambiguous situation even though in a standard Bayesian decision analysis model there should be equivalence between the subjective and objective risk beliefs.

Suppose that there is a two-outcome lottery with success offering utility U and failure offering utility V, where $U > V$. Let the probability of winning the prize be q so that expected utility is $qU + (1-q)V$. The value of expected utility is the same whether q is a precisely specified 'hard' probability or the mean of a subjective probability distribution. One practical complication is that there may be additional risk beliefs that enter beyond that provided by the

---

[9] See Ellsberg (1961) for presentation of this model. Subsequent studies of ambiguity have identified examples of ambiguity-averse behavior as well as cases of ambiguity-seeking behavior. See Camerer and Weber (1992) for a review.

experiment, which can affect risk judgments and the interpretation of the results.[10]

The aversion that respondents exhibit when facing an ambiguous chance of winning a prize has a counterpart when there is an uncertain risk of a loss. Whether people are ambiguity-averse or ambiguity-seeking depends on the level of the mean probability. Suppose that you have been given two medical assessments indicating that you have a possibly fatal form of cancer. For low mean probabilities, ambiguity may be undesirable since the worst-case scenario is that the risk is higher than the mean risk—generating a 'fear' effect. For very high mean risks of death, ambiguity may be desirable since it generates the 'hope' that the risk is lower than the dire mean risk scenario. There is consequently a switch from 'fear' to 'hope' as the mean probability is increased.[11]

People exhibit aversion to ambiguous prospects of environmental losses since those risks tend to be small. A practical example of the presence of risk ambiguity occurs when there are conflicting risk judgments in which the risk experts disagree. How do people process this information?

Suppose people receive two types of risk information, p_1 with precision ξ_1, and p_2 with precision ξ_2. Prior beliefs take the same form as before. The Bayesian probability for the risk of environmental injury will be

$$P(p_1,\xi_1,p_2,\xi_2) = \frac{\gamma q + \xi_1 p_1 + \xi_2 p_2}{\gamma + \xi_1 + \xi_2}. \qquad (2.15)$$

The role of ambiguity, in the sense of the precision of each form of information and the probabilities, enters explicitly.

However, assessed risks in ambiguous risk contexts do not follow this form. Instead there is an additional ambiguity term A that emerges upon estimation or the model, or

---

[10] There are a number of possible explanations for the Ellsberg paradox. One possibility, which is encompassed within the prospective reference theory model, is that the outcomes are defined in terms of success and failure rather than red and black. If one has a perceived prior probability of success for the uncertainty urn that is below 0.5, then the prospect of drawing from urn 1 for which the probability of success is guaranteed with precision to be 0.5 will be higher. This formulation assumes that the mixture of the urn will be manipulated by the operator of the experiment to reduce the probability of success in some manner.

[11] This relationship and the crossover point are explicitly estimated in Viscusi and Chesson (1997).

$$P(p_1,\xi_1,p_2,\xi_2) = \frac{\gamma q + \xi_1 p_1 + \xi_2 p_2}{\gamma + \xi_1 + \xi_2} + A(p_1,\xi_1,p_2,\xi_2). \qquad (2.16)$$

Measures that affected the value of A in the environmental risk experiment described below include the range of the risk estimates and the identity of the information providers. In some specifications of ambiguity models, A may increase the assessed risk of an adverse outcome, but not decrease the assessed risk of a favorable outcome, so that probabilities no longer sum to 1.0.

Table 2.3.   Risk Ambiguity and the Size of the Nerve Disease Risk Spread

Risk levels in area A	Sample size	Median	Mean	Standard error of mean	Minimum (n)	Maximum (n)
(a) Risk ambiguity						
150,200	65	175.00	178.35	1.24	150.50 (1)	200.00 (1)
(b) Size of spread effect						
110,240	58	180.00	191.08	3.95	115.00 (1)	240.00 (13)

Source: Viscusi, Magat, and Huber (1991), table 1.

Table 2.3 summarizes the experimental evidence on subjects' responses to the risks of nerve disease from air pollution exposures arising from toxic chemicals. For panel (a), in which there is some disparity in the views of the experts, one expert considers the risk to be 150 per million and the other expert estimates the risk to be 200 per million. Respondents view this fairly narrow disparity in risk beliefs as being not much different from their mean value of 175, as their average precisely understood risk that they view as equivalent is a nerve disease risk of 178 per million population. Results are starker if there is a mean preserving spread that increases the divergence of the expert risks judgments. In panel (b), one expert believes the risk is 110 and the other believes the risk is 240 per million. In this context, the mean risk assessment is 191 per million, which is significantly different from the midpoint value of 175. Moreover, 13 of the 58 risk respondents assessed the risk as being the upper bound high-risk estimate of 240 per million.

This result reflects a tendency for people to place a greater weight on the worst-case scenario when there are divergences in risk judgments for a small risk of a loss. Risk contexts in which there is substantial disagreement among experts are consequently likely to lead to excessively alarmist responses to risk to the extent that the most shrill risk judgments receive the greatest weight. My recent experimental evidence suggests that this effect is particularly great in situations in which the identity of the experts is different. Disagreement among experts from two different organizations (e.g. government and industry) is likely to lead to a much greater assessed risk than will two differing risk judgments from an identical source.

My experimental results focused on two sources of information on chemical risks—the polluting industry itself and the government.[12] The underlying economic issue is the weight placed on each information source depending on whether it indicated a high or low risk. The average weight on the risks after controlling for the source of the information was not statistically different from 0.5 so that subjects did not always weigh the high risk more. They were not alarmist in general if there was no divergence of the source of risk opinion, e.g. if the source was two government studies. However, if the studies were by two different parties (industry and government), people cut the weight they placed on the low-risk study in half (decreased by 0.24) and increased the weight placed on the high-risk study. The presence of diverse information sources, not simply differences in risk studies alone, contributes to the alarmist reactions to risk.

Conflicting risk policy debates consequently do more than simply cause confusion. They also create the impetus for an excessively alarmist response to risk. Unfortunately, as is shown in Chapter 6, these tendencies are also mirrored in government risk assessment practices.

PUBLICITY REGARDING RISKS

Some of the most heavily publicized risks are the most overestimated.[13] Natural disasters, such as tornadoes and floods, were

[12] The empirical results discussed below are based on Table 1, equation 2, of Viscusi (1997).
[13] Psychologists have noted that the availability of heuristic may help explain this excessive reaction.

among the most prominent overestimated risks in Figure 2.1. Studies have also linked the patterns of overestimation with newspaper coverage. Dramatic risks, such as explosions, tend to be overestimated, as are risks that are outside of individual control.

TABLE 2.4.   How the Public and EPA Rate Health Risks Associated with Environmental Problems

Public	EPA experts
1. Hazardous waste sites	Medium to low
2. Exposure to worksite chemicals	High
3. Industrial pollution of waterways	Low
4. Nuclear accident radiation	Not ranked
5. Radioactive waste	Not ranked
6. Chemical leaks from underground storage tanks	Medium to low
7. Pesticides	High
8. Pollution from industrial accidents	Medium to low
9. Water pollution from farm runoff	Medium
10. Tap water contamination	High
11. Industrial Air Pollution	High
12. Ozone Layer destruction	High
13. Coastal water contamination	Low
14. Sewage-plant water pollution	Medium to low
15. Vehicle exhaust	High
16. Oil spills	Medium to low
17. Acid rain	High
18. Water pollution from urban runoff	Medium
19. Damaged wetlands	Low
20. Genetic alteration	Low
21. Non-hazardous waste sites	Medium to low
22. Greenhouse effect	Low
23. Indoor air pollution	High
24. X-ray radiation	Not ranked
25. Indoor radon	High
26. Microwave oven radiation	Not ranked

Source: Allen (1987), and national opinion polls by the Roper Organization in December 1987 and January 1988.

It is not unexpected then that individual ranking of assessed risks may be driven by factors other than the actual risk levels. Table 2.4 summarizes the public ranking of 26 different environmental risks along with the comparative ranking by experts from the US

Environmental Protection Agency (EPA). The number one risk in the public's view is that from hazardous waste sites. These risks from toxic chemicals received massive television coverage in the United States, particularly with respect to the toxic wastes at a landfill site called Love Canal. Notwithstanding the public's ranking, EPA experts rate the risks as medium to low, and even these risk assessments may be excessive, as will be shown in Chapter 6. Indeed, hazardous waste sites pose an almost negligible risk to human health when compared with the many more fundamental risks we face.

Many less visible and less publicized hazards rank low in the public's estimation, including indoor air pollution and indoor radon, whereas these are ranked high by government officials. Visible risks, dramatic risks, and publicized risks are much more likely to capture the public's attention than are hazards that are less apparent and have received less media attention.

RISK MEASUREMENT CAVEATS

Most of the risk measures discussed in this chapter involved quantitative risk assessments in well defined, probabilistic terms. However, the public risk ratings in Table 2.4 were in terms of whether risks are rated 'high' or 'low,' and much of the risk assessment literature focuses on qualitative perceptions. Does a worker consider a job risky, or do people consider smoking dangerous? One must exercise care in interpreting such measures since differences in risk valuation may influence risk assessment. The value the respondent places on good versus bad health will affect the degree to which some activity is regarded as 'dangerous.'

Table 2.5 summarizes these differences for a sample of chemical workers.[14] The first column is the assessed annual probability of an injury for the worker, and the next three columns report the fraction of workers in each objective risk range who perceive their job as dangerous. For the relatively low risk levels from 0 to 0.05, 50 percent of the college-educated view their jobs as dangerous and 19 percent of the not-college-educated consider the jobs to be dangerous. These differences continue, though they decrease in the higher-risk ranges.

[14] This research, which is joint with Anil Gaba, is based on data reported in Viscusi and O'Connor (1984). See Gaba and Viscusi (1997).

TABLE 2.5.   Quantitative and subjective risk judgments

Quantitative job risk: probability	Fraction perceiving that job is dangerous		
	Full sample	College-educated	Not college-educated
0–0.05	0.33	0.50	0.19
0.06–0.10	0.52	0.68	0.40
0.11–0.15	0.79	0.83	0.76
0.16–0.20	0.75	0.76	0.73
0.21–0.25	1.00	1.00	1.00
0.26–0.30	1.00	1.00	1.00
0.31–0.35	1.00	1.00	1.00

There is consequently a calibration issue with respect to subjective qualitative risk perceptions. Using maximum likelihood methods, it is possible to estimate the cutoff risk probability values for the worker to consider the job risky. These levels are 0.055 for the college-educated and 0.085 for those who are not college-educated. A higher quantitative risk level is needed for those not college-educated to label their job as dangerous. Similar differences are apparent for blue-collar and white-collar workers.

Differences in risk preferences may contaminate differences in expressed subjective risk beliefs. Proper risk assessment questions or recalibration of subjective risk questions can address this difficulty. However, this result highlights a broader task facing those who study risk—the importance of distinguishing the influence of preferences from risk perceptions.

AN OVERVIEW OF RISK PERCEPTION BIASES

Although risk decisions are frequently flawed, they are typically flawed in a systematic manner. People overestimate small identified risks and may ignore small risks of which they are completely ignorant.[15] Similarly, there is a tendency to underestimate many of the large risks we face. The overestimation of highly publicized risks cre-

---

[15] See Kunreuther *et al.* (1978) for discussion of this latter result with respect to natural disasters.

ates not only the potential for alarmist public responses to risk, but also possible pressures on governmental behavior, particularly when these risks are novel and generate an exaggerated public response.

The patterns of choices also may have surprising implications. People may overestimate small risks and respond in an exaggerated way. However, these same patterns of bias imply that people also underestimate the extent of the risk improvement that will occur from their safety precautions. Thus, the perceptional biases can lead to seemingly contradictory behavior—avoiding unsafe products while at the same time failing to exercise appropriate care in the risky activities in which they do engage. This precautionary behavior paradox arises from the difference in the aspects of the risk perception relation that drive these different decisions.

An overriding characteristic of risky choices is that people will have a limited cognitive ability to process information about small risks. Even thinking about what a probability of one in a million means takes us beyond our usual daily experience.

Nevertheless, there are a variety of systematic aspects of decisions that we wish to preserve. For example, virtually all aspects of our diet pose some risks. However, the solution is not for the government to override our differences in preferences and mandate the same food intake for all. Rather, we regulate some risks and provide information with respect to others in an effort to foster relatively safe choices that are simultaneously reflective of individual preferences. The role of these different institutional responses is the subject of the subsequent chapters.

3
Hazard Warnings and Risk Information

If people do not have accurate risk perceptions, the obvious direct solution is to provide information to remedy this market failure. So long as people can learn and act upon their new knowledge, there is the prospect of addressing the source of the inadequacy.

This seemingly straightforward approach has long been resisted by government officials. The widely held view among regulators has been that information programs are ineffective in altering behavior.[1] As a result, more direct intervention is needed through regulatory action. This pessimistic assessment of the efficacy of information programs is often driven by self-interest, as it leads to an outcome that fosters the agenda of regulators wishing to expand their domain.

Many risk information efforts have not had success since they simply reminded people of what they already knew. The information did not alter their risk judgments. This chapter explores the potential role of risk information and the economic mechanisms through which this information operates.

RATIONALE FOR HAZARD WARNINGS

The 1970s was the era in which government policy focused on direct regulation of risk and the environment. The 1980s marked the emergence of hazard warnings as a prominent policy alternative. Recognition of the importance of personal risk protection and risk-taking decisions has led to increasing emphasis on right-to-know policies, efforts that promote an informed citizenry, and recognition of individuals' ability and right to make choices to protect their own lives. The contexts in which risk information has become instrumen-

[1] See Adler and Pittle (1984) and Wagenaar (1992).

tal range from information on job-related chemical exposures and established efforts such as cigarette warnings, to more novel risk communication efforts such as the provision of information to assist public debates regarding hazardous waste cleanups.

There are a variety of rationales for using hazard warnings as the chosen form of regulatory intervention. If the market failure is a lack of information, then warnings can address this limitation directly. In terms of the model in Chapter 2, warning information that conveys an accurate risk probability in a sufficiently convincing way will lead individuals to have sound risk beliefs.

More specifically, let q_i be the person's initial assessed risk of outcome i and let p_i be the risk conveyed by the warning. Unless p_i exceeds q_i, the warning will not increase risk beliefs. However, what appears to be most influential in practice is the degree of informational content associated with the warning. Warnings that have high values of ξ relative to the weight γ on prior beliefs will be more effective in shifting risk beliefs. The credibility of the risk message is of enormous practical consequence.

Warnings policies also play an essential role in situations in which there are decentralized decisions. Often it is not possible for regulators to monitor our actions that are related to risk. For example, government officials cannot go into people's homes to ensure that households are handling dangerous chemicals properly. They can, however, provide consumers with information that ideally will assist them in making sensible decisions on their own.

A particularly disturbing example of hazard warnings for decentralized decisions is the unprecedented set of warnings currently provided by the Hertz car rental dealership at the Miami International Airport.[2] Because of the rash of car hijackings and foreign tourist murders in the Miami area, Hertz provides all those renting cars with a map indicating the safe highways with a 'Sun Symbol,' a 12-page flier with a series of 18 different warnings in six different languages called 'Safety Tips,'[3] and a written waiver that must be signed by the car renter acknowledging that Hertz has provided this safety information. Clearly, Hertz is unable to monitor where drivers take their

---

[2] These warnings appear to have been stimulated by liability concerns so as to avoid lawsuits after car-jackings.

[3] For example, safety tip number 13 is: 'If your car is bumped from behind in a secluded or dark area, do not pull over and stop. Drive to the nearest public area and call for police assistance.'

cars and how they choose to drive. However, through this set of warnings, the firm has communicated the distinctive nature of the risks that threaten drivers in this area and has provided a comprehensive set of behavioral rules for decreasing the risk. Direct regulation would not have been feasible, given the decentralized nature of driver decisions.

Apart from these rationales, there is also a political impetus for informational policies in that they provide an intermediate policy option. Policies that either must permit an unfettered use of a product or ban the product altogether represent extreme policy alternatives. In situations in which there is heterogeneity in the risk level or in risk preferences, banning a product may deprive many consumers of a beneficial new product in the effort to address problems associated with a minority of consumers. As a practical matter, information often plays a constructive role in giving policymakers an intermediate policy option when there is insufficient evidence to warrant direct regulation, but enough concern about a potential risk to alert the public of the need for care.

RISK BELIEFS AND DISCRETE CHOICES

Risk communication policies operate in two general contexts. One potential role is to affect individual beliefs concerning the riskiness of an activity or a product and thus to influence the discrete decision of whether or not to engage in such a pursuit. Hazard warnings consequently influence our choices of which jobs to take, which products to consume, and which activities to pursue. However, there is a second role of warnings as well, which is to influence our behavior within these activities. Workplace warnings may urge the use of protective equipment, and the warnings for consumer products may advise the use of bicycle helmets or care while skiing or scuba diving.[4]

The two types of evidence with respect to the impact of warnings involve structured experiments and natural experiments. Table 3.1 reports the results of a structured experiment in which we gave four

---

[4] It is noteworthy that at the time of these lectures there was a large scale public information campaign to encourage children to use helmets in Scandinavia. In Lund, Sweden, which was the site of these lectures, the McDonald's restaurant placemats featured a cartoon in which Ronald McDonald urged children to adopt sensible behavior while riding bikes by wearing a bicycle helmet.

TABLE 3.1.   Means of Variables for Each Labeling Group

Risk variable	Sodium bicarbonate ($n = 31$)	Lachrymator ($n = 106$)	Asbestos ($n = 102$)	TNT ($n = 96$)
Baseline risk	0.12	0.10	0.09	0.10
Risk after receiving warning	0.06	0.18	0.26	0.31
Risk premium required after receiving warning of increased risk (1995 dollar rate)[a]	0.00	$3,032	$4,733	$8,150
Fraction of workers wishing to quit after warning	0.00	0.23	0.65	0.73
Fraction of workers willing to take the job again after warning	0.90	0.58	0.11	0.07

[a] The risk premium figures are conditional upon facing an increased risk and being willing to accept a finite risk premium.

Source: adapted from Viscusi and O'Connor (1984).

different groups of chemical workers a hazard warning for a chemical. The survey informed each worker receiving the warning that the labelled chemical would replace the chemicals with which the individual currently worked. The four possible labels were sodium bicarbonate (i.e., household baking soda), chloroacetophenome (a lachrymator that makes workers cry and is an eye irritant), asbestos, and TNT.

Table 3.1 summarizes the effect of each warning on each worker group. The worker's baseline risk assessment appears in the first row of the table. Workers assessed the job risk probability using a linear injury frequency scale for which the average US injury rate was the anchor. The range of the average assessed prior risks for the four subsamples was from an equivalent annual probability of job injury of 0.09 to 0.12. After receiving this labeling information, workers who received the sodium bicarbonate label decreased their assessed risk assessment from 0.12 to 0.06. Being told that household baking soda would replace the chemicals with which they now worked had a favorable effect on risk beliefs. The other warnings of hazards increased workers' assessed risks where these risk perceptions after the information acquisition ranged from 0.18 to 0.31.

The usual market model since the time of Adam Smith is that workers will require a compensating differential to incur the added risk, which is the observed result. This risk premium ranges from $3,032 for the lachrymator to $8,150 for TNT (1995 dollars).

If workers are not paid a wage increase, they should respond in some manner. The results indicate that, although no workers would quit the safe sodium bicarbonate job without a wage increase, 65 percent would quit the job with asbestos exposures and 73 percent would quit the job with TNT exposures. Similarly, workers' willingness to take the job again without a wage increase would diminish to 11 percent for asbestos and 7 percent for TNT exposures. Hazard warnings consequently create a multiplicity of market responses arising from increasing risk perceptions. These responses include workers' willingness to stay on the job and the terms of tradeoff they demand for remaining at that position.

The importance of informational content in driving risk perception differences is exemplified in the results for the hazard warnings considered earlier in this chapter. Both the prior risk assessment q_i and the risk level implied by the warning p_i are consequential. Using information on the individual's prior and posterior risk assessments, it is possible to estimate the relative precision ξ/γ of the information content of the warning relative to the worker's prior risk beliefs. More specifically, break a variant of equation (2.1) into component terms, or

$$\text{Perceived product risk } P_i = \frac{\gamma q_i}{\gamma + \xi} + \frac{\xi p_i}{\gamma + \xi}. \qquad (3.1)$$

In a regression of the perceived product risk (the dependent variable) on the initial assessed risk of the job q_i, one can write (3.1) in terms of the observable probability values—the posterior risk dependent variable P_i and the prior risk q_i—and a constant term a_i, a coefficient β_i, and a random error term ϵ_i, or

$$P_i = a_i + \beta_i q_i + \epsilon_i. \qquad (3.2)$$

The coefficient of q_i, which we will call β_i, is the relative information weight attached to the prior, $\gamma/(\gamma + \xi)$. The value of the implied risk

p_i is not observed. As a result, the estimation captures the value of the second term in (3.1) through a constant term α_i which varies by chemical and reflects the combined influence of the various components $\xi p_i/(\gamma + \xi)$.

The estimates of the parameters α_i and β_i provide the key information regarding the character of the warnings effort since the underlying characteristics of the warning can be expressed in terms of these estimated values. The parameters estimated directly give the fraction of the information weight placed on the γ prior, or β_i, and the value of the job risk probability weighted by its relative informational content, or α_i. In particular, one can estimate the risk level p_i implied by the warning, where

$$p_i = \alpha_i/(\beta_i - 1). \tag{3.3}$$

Similarly, one can derive the relative weight placed on the information in the hazard warning as compared with the person's prior beliefs, or

$$\xi_i/\gamma = (1/\beta_i) - 1. \tag{3.4}$$

As the results in Table 3.2 indicate, the estimated implied risks p_i from the warning were fairly high for all chemicals other than sodium bicarbonate. However, the relative informational content differed starkly and was often influential. The relative informational content of the warning compared with the prior was low for the unfamiliar chemical that was a lachrymator and 31 times as influential as the prior beliefs for the TNT warning—a highly familiar explosive. The mechanisms of the learning process—in particular, the informational content as well as the implied risk value—determine the ultimate economic effects of warnings. The asbestos and TNT warnings were particularly effective, not simply because they conveyed the

TABLE 3.2   Estimated Characteristics of the Hazard Warnings

	Implied warning risk p_i	Relative weight on warning information ξ_i/γ
Sodium bicarbonate	0.04	3.7
Lachrymator	0.24	1.3
Asbestos	0.29	6.4
TNT	0.32	31.4

highest risk level, but also because they had a higher informational content. In these instances, the relative informational content for asbestos was 6.4 and for TNT was 31.4, whereas the informational content for the lachrymator/chloroacetophenome warning, which had much vaguer properties, was only 1.3.

THE CIGARETTE WARNINGS EXPERIENCE

Perhaps the most highly publicized large scale individual risk is that posed by cigarettes. In the United States, this product has been the subject of three decades of on-product labeling, annual reports by the US Surgeon General regarding smoking hazards, and bans on various forms of cigarette advertising. Canada and many Western European nations have also adopted vigorous warning efforts pertaining to smoking, along with advertising restrictions and limitations on the character of cigarette packaging.

Concern that smoking is a risky activity is not misplaced. As

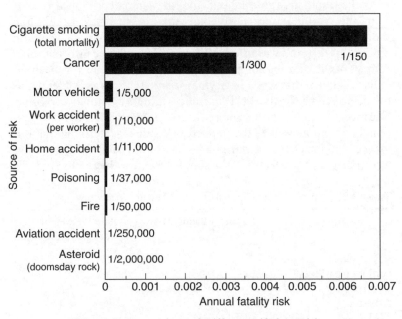

FIG. 3.1 Comparison of Different Lifetime Risks

Figure 3.1 indicates, the risks of smoking are substantial and dwarf most other hazards we face. The annual risk of death for a smoker is 1/150, which is double the annual risk of death from cancer from all causes and more than an order of magnitude greater than risks such as those posed by motor vehicle accidents and work accidents.

A particularly noteworthy entry in Figure 3.1 is the risk of being killed by an asteroid. One consensus scientific estimate is that there is a probability of 1/500,000 that the Earth will be struck by a dooms-day rock, posing an annual risk of death to any given individual of 1/2,000,000.[5] Not surprisingly, there has been a divergence of scien-tific opinion regarding the magnitude of the risk. Indeed, scientists at Cornell University, who sought to obtain government funding for their research on rockets that will destroy such an asteroid, estimated the risk to be as high as 1/6,000.[6] If this estimate is to be believed, the annual risk of being killed by an asteroid is greater than the risk of being killed at work. One clearly desirable policy option is to invest in refining such widely disparate risk estimates before diverting sub-stantial resources to this protective task.

A more solidly established target of government concern is smok-ing. Table 3.3 summarizes the different eras of hazard warnings for cigarettes in the United States. These warnings were on-product labels on the side of cigarette packages, which were also required to be included in cigarette print and billboard advertising. These prod-uct-specific warnings have been accompanied by other informational efforts as well, such as a ban on television and radio ads.

In conjunction with a variety of public education efforts, these var-ious information campaigns have contributed to a dampening of the growth of cigarette consumption in the United States. As is shown in Figure 3.2, cigarette consumption was on the rise through the first half of this century, after which it plateaued and has subsequently decreased. It is also noteworthy that the major dip in smoking in the early 1950s occurred after the release of an adverse Mayo Clinic report on cigarette smoking, which received substantial publicity.

Although these statistics reflect an impressive reversal of the upward trend in smoking, the even greater influence has been with respect to changes in the types of cigarette smoked. Figure 3.3 sketches the trend in per capita cigarette consumption as well as the trend in tar-adjusted per capita cigarette consumption. For con-

---

[5] *The Economist* (Sept. 11, 1993), p. 13.
[6] *New York Times* (June 18, 1991), p. B5.

TABLE 3.3.   Cigarette Warning Content Summaries

Warning period	Warning content[a]
1965	'Caution: Cigarette Smoking May Be Hazardous to Your Health.'
1969	'Warning: The Surgeon General Has Determined That Cigarette Smoking Is Dangerous to Your Health.'
1984	1. 'SURGEON GENERAL'S WARNING: Smoking Causes Lung Cancer, Heart Disease, Emphysema, and May Complicate Pregnancy.' 2. 'SURGEON GENERAL'S WARNING: Quitting Smoking Now Greatly Reduces Serious Risks to Your Health.' 3. 'SURGEON GENERAL'S WARNING: Smoking by Pregnant Women May Result in Fetal Injury, Premature Birth, and Low Birth Weight.' 4. 'SURGEON GENERAL'S WARNING: Cigarette Smoke Contains Carbon Monoxide.'

[a] All warnings wording is specified by legislation. See 15 U. S. C. §§1331–41 (1982).

creteness, the starting point for each series has been normalized relative to 1944. Per capita cigarette consumption displayed an upward drift that stabilized in the 1960s and has been declining since the mid-1970s. In contrast, the tar-adjusted cigarette consumption has dropped by more than two-thirds over the past half century. The smoking literature has focused primarily on the effect of information on the discrete choice of whether to smoke and the quantity of cigarettes smoked. There has been comparatively little attention paid to the safety precautions adopted while smoking—the choice of the cigarette tar level. There has been a much greater shift in the kind of cigarettes people smoke than in the number of cigarettes. Thus, hazard warnings affect not only the decision to engage in the risky activity but also the nature of the risks one takes within the context of these activities.

These changes in smoking activity have also been accompanied by shifts on public perceptions of smoking. Reflective of these changes in beliefs is the stark change in public attitudes toward environmen-

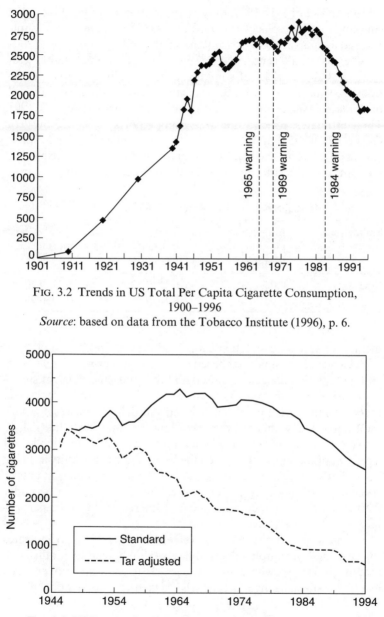

Fig. 3.2 Trends in US Total Per Capita Cigarette Consumption,
1900–1996
Source: based on data from the Tobacco Institute (1996), p. 6.

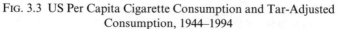

Fig. 3.3 US Per Capita Cigarette Consumption and Tar-Adjusted
Consumption, 1944–1994

tal tobacco smoke. In 1977, only 16 percent of the public favored no smoking in public places, whereas by 1988, 60 percent of the public favored a complete ban on smoking in all public places.[7]

Whereas a half century ago there was not as much public consciousness of the risks of smoking, current individual risk perceptions are substantial. Table 3.4 indicates various estimates of the risk of smoking based on the state of information in 1985 and 1991. These estimates, which I prepared using reports by the US Surgeon General, indicate that in 1985 the lung cancer mortality risk to smokers was 0.05–0.10, the total mortality risk was just over triple that amount, and the total mortality risk to society including environ-

TABLE 3.4.   Actual Smoking Risk Ranges, 1985 and 1991

Survey year	Lung cancer mortality risk to smoker	Total mortality risk to smoker	Total mortality risk to society
1985	0.05–0.10	0.16–0.32	0.21–0.42
1991	0.06–0.13	0.18–0.36	0.23–0.46

mental tobacco smoke, fetal deaths, and fires was a bit greater.

Evidence I have analyzed based on a national survey for 1985 suggests that the public generally assessed the lung cancer risk of smoking to be 0.43, with smokers assessing the risk at 0.37. In each case, the lung cancer risk component is substantially overassessed, with the total risk assessment even exceeding the total mortality risk to smokers. Equally noteworthy is that only 5 percent of the public and 9 percent of the smokers assessed the lung cancer probability as being below 0.05 and just under 10 percent of the total population and 15 percent of the smoking population estimated the risk to be under 0.10. The extent of underassessment of the risk seems to be particularly small.

My more recent survey evidence reported in Table 3.5 indicates that for the full sample of respondents the lung cancer fatality risk assessment is 0.38, where this value is 0.31 for current smokers. The assessed total smoking mortality risk is greater, with a value of 0.54

---

[7] These results are from Gallup poll surveys for the respective years, where the complete results are reported in table 3-3 of Viscusi (1992*b*).

TABLE 3.5.   Smoking Fatality Risk Perceptions[a]

Sample	Mean (standard error of the mean)	
	Lung cancer fatality risk	Total smoking mortality risk
Full sample	0.38 (0.02)	0.54 (0.07)
Current smokers	0.31 (0.04)	0.47 (0.05)
Current nonsmokers	0.40 (0.02)	0.56 (0.03)
Former	0.36 (0.03)	0.50 (0.04)
Never	0.42 (0.03)	0.59 (0.03)

[a] Sample size = 206.

for the full sample and 0.47 for current smokers. Each of these values exceeds the upper bound of the scientific assessments of the total smoking mortality risk to smokers.

The overassessment of smoking risks does not appear to be a size-related bias. Smoking risks are sufficiently large so as not to qualify as a small overassessed risk. The substantial publicity given to smoking hazards appears largely responsible. Since the character of the anti-smoking efforts is to note that smoking is risky rather than to convey a particular risk probability, the main effect of the smoking risk information campaigns has been to raise risk perceptions rather than to foster convergence to the true estimated risk level.

The variation in smoking risk perceptions across the population is of considerable interest as well. If p is the prior risk assessment, q_1 is the risk implied by the individual's smoking experience, q_2 is the risk implied by hazard warnings, and the informational content parameters are specified as before, then,

$$\text{Perceived risk } P = \frac{\gamma p + \xi_1 q_1 + \xi_2 q_2}{\gamma + \xi_1 + \xi_2}. \tag{3.5}$$

If warning risk information q_2 suggests a higher risk probability than the value of $(\gamma p + \xi_1 q_1)/(\gamma + \xi_1)$, then it will increase risk beliefs.

Thus, on an empirical basis, one might expect anti-smoking warnings to raise risk beliefs. One possible exception is the warning proposed in 1995 for public comment by the US Food and Drug Administration but which was not adopted. The proposal was to indicate that one out of three smokers die from smoking. That risk level is considerably below current risk beliefs and might depress risk beliefs.

Smokers are expected to have lower risk beliefs wholly apart from their self-selected status. If smoking activity conveys a risk level q_1 to smokers that is below the warning risk q_2, then it will dilute the effect of warnings in the weighted informational average in equation (3.5).

Younger smokers are particularly likely to assess high risks since such a substantial fraction of their risk information has come in the post-warnings era. The effect of warnings information is to increase risk beliefs, so that

$$\partial P / \partial \xi_2 > 0 \tag{3.6}$$

whenever $q_2 > p, q_1$. However, the extent of this effect dampens over time, or

$$\partial^2 P / \partial \xi_2^2 < 0. \tag{3.7}$$

There should consequently be a dampening of the effect of warnings with age.

The lung cancer risk perception results in Table 3.6 bear out these various predictions. Nonsmokers have higher risk perceptions than current or former smokers. This pattern is borne out for every age group in Table 3.6. Moreover, current smokers always have the lowest risk perceptions, followed by former smokers, and then non-smokers in every case except the youngest age group—for which the difference between current and former smokers was not statistically significant. Risk perceptions rise as the fraction of information received in the post-warnings era increases. The youngest age group (age 16–21) has the highest risk beliefs, or a perceived lung cancer risk of 0.49. These risk perception amounts decrease for the older age groups to a value of 0.42 for those age 22–45 and an almost identical value for those age 46+.

Empirical evidence also indicates that these risk perceptions have a significant negative effect on the discrete smoking decisions which does not differ significantly by age. Indeed, the average US excise tax on cigarettes of 31 percent of the retail price per pack decreases

TABLE 3.6. Variations in Lung Cancer Risk Perceptions with Age and Smoking Status

| Age group | Mean risk, by group[a] | | | |
	Current smoker	Former smoker	Nonsmoker	All respondents in age group
Age 16–21	0.445	0.429	0.511	0.490
	(0.043)	(0.037)	(0.017)	(0.015)
Age 22–45	0.382	0.390	0.454	0.417
	(0.011)	(0.013)	(0.010)	(0.006)
Age 46+	0.328	0.421	0.456	0.418
	(0.017)	(0.015)	(0.011)	(0.008)
All ages	0.368	0.408	0.464	0.426
	(0.009)	(0.010)	(0.007)	(0.005)

[a] Standard error of mean in parentheses.

smoking demand by less than half as much as the effect of smoking risk perceptions.[8] In the current era of hazard warnings and extensive smoking risk information, individuals not only appear to be aware of the risk but seem to overassess it. These risk perceptions in turn affect smoking behavior.

This evidence alone does not imply that smoking decisions are fully rational. Nor does evidence of overassessment of the risk imply that current hazard communication efforts have been excessively zealous. It is difficult to achieve pinpoint optimality with respect to hazard warnings. What is clear is that the combination of societal efforts to convey the importance of smoking risks has had a dramatic effect in influencing this risky behavior and has led to a situation in which risks seem to be reasonably well understood.

GENERALIZING FROM THE CIGARETTE EXPERIENCE

Policymakers' natural inclination has been to attempt to imitate the

---

[8] More specifically, the cigarette tax effect is the same as a lung cancer risk perception of 0.17 (using demand elasticity of –0.4), and the average lung cancer risk perception is 0.43. See Viscusi (1992*b*), especially p. 109.

success of cigarette warnings in other policy contexts. One such effort took place in the state of California with respect to hazardous chemicals in food. The warning contemplated by regulators pertained to many product risks that exceeded a lifetime cancer risk threshold of 1/100,000 over a 70-year life time of exposure. This risk level involved an annual risk of 1/7,000,000, which is below the scientific consensus estimate that we will be killed by an asteroid.

Notwithstanding the negligible level of risks, the proposed wording was: 'WARNING: The State of California has determined that this product causes cancer.' Officials patterned this warning after the 1969 cigarette warning (see Table 3.3). Not surprisingly, test subjects viewing this warning considered any product bearing such a label to be almost as risky as cigarettes. Indeed, the average person assessing this warning rated the risk as equivalent to 0.4 pack of cigarettes—a consumption activity that poses enormously greater risks.[9]

The market response to hazard warnings is evident not only for cigarettes, but also for other products. Consumption of products containing artificial sweeteners such as saccharin declined after the advent of saccharin warnings. Even in situations in which the recipient group for the warning is a learned intermediary bringing to bear advanced expertise, there is an evident impact of hazard warnings. A widely used pharmaceutical product in the United States was tetracycline, which continues to be the drug of choice for ailments such as Rocky Mountain spotted fever and lyme disease. The unfortunate consequence of this drug is that it causes tooth staining for children under the age of 9, who are forming their permanent teeth. In 1963 companies introduced information pertaining to the tooth staining hazard into the hazard warning section of the patient package insert. As is shown in Figure 3.4, tetracycline use has continued to increase for the population group aged 9 and above that was not affected by the warning, whereas the targeted warning group greatly diminished its use of the product. In this as in other instances, well designed warning policies have played an instrumental role in influencing potentially risky decisions.

[9] In practice, the implementation of this regulation has not led to severe consequences. For example, many companies have reformulated their products. One such reformulated product is Liquid Paper. One consumer product that has received the warning is sand for children's sandboxes, which could not be reformulated to eliminate all potential hazardous chemicals. The state of California also proposed comparable warnings for all products associated with birth defects, where a strict application of the initial proposed warnings would have led to on-product warnings for all products containing caffeine, including coffee, tea, and cola beverages.

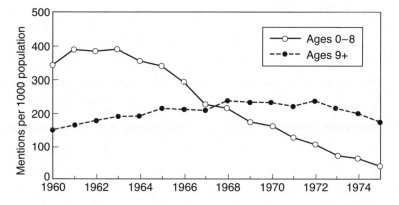

FIG. 3.4 Use of Tetracycline, as Measured by Mentions (Prescriptions and Renewals), 1960–1975

WARNINGS AND PRECAUTIONS

In some cases, the task of warnings is to influence not the choice of an activity, but rather the precautions one takes within that activity. Warnings that increase the perceived probability of injury from product misuse or which provide information on how to decrease this risk can be effective. However, even effective warnings that lead to accurate risk beliefs may not alter behavior if, for example, the individual considers the precaution to be unduly onerous. Table 3.7 summarizes how different precautionary behaviors respond to the presence of hazard warnings for bleach. The most prominent hazard of bleach is that mixing bleach with ammonia or ammonia-based products will form chloramine gas, which is the leading non-suicidal cause of poisonings among adults in the United States and in Europe. The products tested include a label in which the warning information was eliminated, labels for the Clorox brand of bleach and the Brite brand of bleach that are nationally marketed in the United States, and a 'Test' label designed by our warnings research project team to convey the information in an effective manner.

The presence of a warning increases the fraction of respondents who would not mix bleach with toilet bowl cleaner even if the toilet was badly stained by 24 percent, and it leads an additional 16 percent of respondents to avoid adding bleach to ammonia-based cleaners

TABLE 3.7.   Effects of Labels on Precaution-Taking

| Precaution | % of respondents taking precaution | | | | Maximum incremental effect |
	No warning ($n = 51$)	Clorox ($n = 59$)	Brite ($n = 42$)	Test ($n = 44$)	
1. Do not mix bleach with toilet bowl cleaner (if toilet is badly stained)	16	23	36	40	24
2. Do not add bleach to ammonia-based cleaners (for particularly dirty jobs)	69	68	69	84	16
3. Store bleach in childproof location	43	63	50	76	33

Source: Viscusi and Magat (1987), table 4.2.

even for particularly dirty jobs. Warning labels also increase the fraction of respondents who would store the product in a childproof location by 33 percent.

Table 3.8 reports analogous results for drain openers. In addition to the no warning option and a test label, a third label patterned after the nationally marketed Drano and Red Devil Lye also was included in the experiment, where this label includes such a concentration of warnings information that it is the most effective of the labels tested. Once again, hazard warnings have a significant effect on precautionary behavior, increasing the fraction who wear rubber gloves by 19 percent and the storage of the product in a childproof location by 20 percent for households with children under age 5.

In this and other instances, labels are not fully effective. Not all individuals will take the recommended precaution. However, the failure of some people to wear rubber gloves, for example, should not necessarily be viewed as an inadequacy in individual decisions. The same survey also elicited information with respect to individual disutility associated with the precautionary behavior. For quite reason-

TABLE 3.8.　Effect of Warnings on Precautions Taken with Drain Openers

Precaution	% of sample taking precaution			Maximum incremental effect (%)
	Drano Red Devil Lye label	Test label	No warning	
Wear rubber gloves	82	73	63	19
Store in childproof location:				
Households with children under 5	90	83	70	20
Households with no children under 5	63	61	48	15

Source: Viscusi and Magat (1987), tables 4.3 and 4.6, and calculations by the author.

able values of the risk probabilities and the disutilities, it would not necessarily be irrational to forgo the types of precaution listed. Men, for example, are particularly adverse to wearing rubber gloves when performing household chemical chores and are less likely to respond to the urging of the warning.[10]

PRINCIPLES FOR HAZARD WARNINGS POLICY

These results in no way imply that warnings can remedy all informational inadequacies. However, a well designed information effort can play a constructive role in fostering sounder risk decisions.

Perhaps the main prerequisite for an effective warnings policy is that it provide new information in a convincing manner. In terms of the informational formulation in Chapter 2, for information to be new the risk conveyed by the warning must be different from the risk probability that the individual holds initially. Otherwise, risk beliefs are not altered. The information also must be convincing, which means that the informational content term ξ must be high relative to

---

[10] As Wagenaar (1992) has noted, what people say they will do is not always what they actually do. In Magat and Viscusi (1992) we corroborated the experimental precautions with a survey on actual precautionary behavior and found a close correspondence for our consumer survey instrument.

the value of the informational content of associated with prior risk beliefs γ.

An essential concern in designing effective warnings policies is to recognize that individuals have cognitive limitations. Individuals must receive the warnings message, process it, and then act upon it. The structure, format, and content of warnings consequently play an instrumental role in the effect warnings policies have. Boxing the warnings and exhibiting them in a bolder print size may matter up to a point, but the effects of such nuances appear to be diminishing once a reasonable degree of readability has been achieved.

In thinking about hazard warnings, one should conceptualize the entire hazard communication system. Focusing on only a single risk of the product while neglecting others will not promote a reasonable response to risk. Lift trucks, for example, pose roughly three dozen types of fatality risk to the driver or others. Operating motor vehicles such as cars also poses a multiplicity of hazards. On-product labels are often not sufficient. Television ads, advice of a physician, required certified training programs, and licensing of drivers also may be integral parts of an effective hazard communication system.

Perhaps somewhat surprisingly, standardization is often desirable. Contrary to the economists' usual urging that there be a diversity of responses, in this instance uniformity in the warnings vocabulary and in the warnings approach is a desirable feature. International standardization is also desirable for countries in which international trade or a diversity of worker nationalities is consequential. By having a common format, individuals will be more readily able to locate hazard warning information. Moreover, standardizing various warning symbols, such as that for poisoning, as well as human hazard signal words, such as 'danger', 'warning', and 'caution', will give these urgings a comparable meaning which recipients could interpret more reliably.

A final principle for effective warnings is that overwarning is dangerous. Excessive warning distorts relative product comparisons and threatens the credibility of the information provider. The task of information policy is to promote correct risk-taking decisions, not to distort the underlying probabilities and discourage efficient risk-taking behavior.

4
The Value of Life

Perhaps the most sensitive and fundamental aspect of risk policies is establishing a value for human life. More specifically, the quest is not to value certain deaths: rather, it is to assign a rate of tradeoff for statistical lives in some metric, where the typical metric chosen by economists is money.

Even raising this question appears to many to be offensive. However, much of the discomfort arises from a misunderstanding of the task. The search for an economic value of life is not a financial accounting concept. Nor does it reflect the price we would pay to avoid certain death. Rather, it reflects the tradeoffs we are willing to make between very small risks of death and money. We make numerous such tradeoffs daily, whether it is traveling to work in a compact car or eating food that poses a minor risk of cancer and heart disease.

A useful starting point for thinking about value-of-life issues is to consider how much you value your own life. Suppose that you were faced with a 1/10,000 risk of death. This is a one-time-only risk that will not be repeated. The death is immediate and painless. The magnitude of this probability is comparable to the annual occupational fatality risk facing a typical American worker and about half the annual risk of being killed in a motor vehicle accident. If you faced such a risk, how much would you pay to eliminate it?

Table 4.1 summarizes different potential answers to this question. In a series of presentations of this question to students and other audiences, nobody has ever indicated a willingness to pay an infinite amount to eliminate this small risk. This absence of an unbounded commitment to eliminating a minor hazard demonstrates that the value that people attach to their lives is not infinite. The main question is deciding how finite this amount is.

The first column in the table summarizes different possible response levels, and the second column gives the corresponding value of a statistical life. These value-of-life numbers represent the rate of tradeoff implied by the responses in column 1. We can derive these

TABLE 4.1.   Value of Life for Different
Willingness-to-Pay Amounts

Amount will pay	Value of life (dollars)
Infinite	Infinity
above $1,000	at least 10,000,000
$500–1,000	5,000,000–10,000,000
$200–500	2,000,000–5,000,000
$50–200	500,000–2,000,000
0–$50	0–500,000

numbers in two different ways. The first is to recognize that these amounts simply represent the price per unit risk. Consider a respondent who said that $500 was the appropriate amount to eliminate this risk. Then the value per unit risk would be $500 divided by the probability, which is 1/10,000, yielding a value-of-life estimate of $5 million. A more intuitive approach is to imagine a group of 10,000 people, such as an audience in a stadium. Suppose that one of these people would be expected to die. If there was one expected statistical death from this large audience of 10,000 participants, and if each of the participants is willing to pay $500 to eliminate the risk, then it would be possible to raise $5 million collectively from this audience to eliminate the one statistical death to the group, thus establishing the value of life. Such survey questions involving hypothetical risks do not always yield reliable responses, as one difficulty is that people may not truly believe that they face the stated risk. However, they serve as a useful thought process for thinking about what economists' estimates of value of life mean.

Most estimates of the value of life have utilized labor market data to estimate the tradeoff that workers make between job risks and additional pay. Consumer risk studies and contingent valuation (i.e. survey) studies also have addressed value-of-life issues, though the labor market studies are most prevalent.[1]

The basic idea of these studies is that hazardous jobs will command a compensating differential. Since the time of Adam Smith, economists have observed that risky jobs must be attractive in some

---

[1] See Viscusi (1992*a*, 1993*b*) for a review. Also see Jones-Lee (1974, 1989), Jones-Lee and Loomes (1995), and Gerking, de Haan, and Schulze (1988) for survey evidence and Kniesner and Leeth (1995) for an international perspective.

other way, such as higher pay, for workers to be willing to bear the risk. Elephant handlers at the Philadelphia Zoo receive $1,000 extra per year because elephants are said to pose an extra risk to handlers they don't like. Fire fighters in Kuwait received $500,000 per year, much of which no doubt was due to the substantial risks incurred in this job.

There are, of course, notable exceptions. People pay as much as $65,000 for the opportunity to be part of an expedition to climb Mount Everest. The death rate for this adventure is considerable—roughly 150 deaths, compared with the total of 600 climbers who have made it to the top.[2] Such behavior is attractive because its 'compensating differential' is in terms of the exhilaration and sense of accomplishment from a successful climb.

Studies of risk tradeoffs have focused primarily not on these attractive risky pursuits but on the more mundane hazards of risky jobs and products. More formal examinations of compensating differential theory have involved detailed statistical tests to distinguish the premium for risk, controlling for other factors. Wage studies in the United States as well as many other countries, such as the United Kingdom, Canada, Japan, and Australia, have documented significant job risk premiums. The average risks faced by workers are now 1/10,000 for the typical worker and 1/1,000 for workers in very high risk jobs. Using these data, economists have estimated compensation for these risks that cluster in the $3 million–$7 million range, with an average value of $5 million. These values in turn provide the basis for pricing statistical lives in benefit–cost analysis studies. Such analyses are so widespread that they are used more by non-economists than economists.

Figure 4.1 illustrates the methodology underlying these studies. Firms are willing to offer higher pay for riskier jobs because additional safety improvements to make the job safer are costly. Moreover, since the costs of safety are generally increasing, the cost savings from increasing risks will be decreasing. Thus, for one firm the offer curve in Figure 4.1 might be *FF*, whereas for another firm the offer curve might be *GG*. The opportunity set for workers consists of the outer envelope of these market opportunities since jobs offering lower pay for the same risk are dominated by more remunerative jobs. In this instance, however, Figure 4.1 illustrates only two potential job offers for simplicity.

[2] 'Death on the Highest Peak,' *New York Times*, May 18, 1997, sect. 4, p. 2.

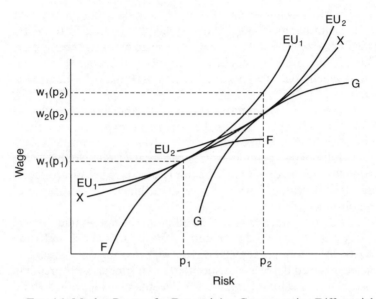

FIG. 4.1 Market Process for Determining Compensating Differentials

On the labor supply side of the market, worker 1 has a constant expected utility locus EU_1, and worker 2 has a constant expected utility locus EU_2. These are the expected utility loci that are tangent to the most attractive market opportunities available to each of the workers. The indifference map set for each worker displays increasing preference as one moves in a north-westerly direction. The curves EU_1 and EU_2 have a positive slope since additional pay is required to face increasing risk. The economic assumptions required for this result are minimal: one will only need to prefer not being injured to being injured.[3]

Worker 1 selects point p_1 and associated wage $w_1(p_1)$, whereas worker 2 selects risk p_2 with a wage $w_2(p_2)$. Based on these two observed wage–risk pairs, economists will fit a curve such as XX to trace out these observed market tangencies. Thus, the estimated wage–risk tradeoffs will reflect a variety of different market tradeoff rates for different workers rather than estimating a particular indi-

[3] For example, it is not necessary that subjects be risk-averse with respect to monetary lotteries to obtain this result. There are, however, some other minor restrictions; see Viscusi (1979).

vidual's constant expected utility locus or any particular firm's offer curve.

Knowledge of the average wage–risk tradeoff for the market will prove to be instructive in establishing measures of local tradeoffs with respect to very small changes in risk. However, one should be careful in extrapolating these findings for large risk changes. For example, if one would require that worker 1 incur job risk p_2, it would not be sufficient to give that worker $w_2(p_2)$ to keep the worker on the same constant expected utility locus. As is shown in Figure 4.1, the required wage compensation would be $w_1(p_2)$, which is greater.

By necessity, market-based data are limited to analyzing local tradeoffs. However, this shortcoming does not mean that we could never obtain estimates of the shape of worker preferences. By using data from the hazard warning study for workers discussed in Chapter 3, for example, it is possible to estimate not only the constant expected utility locus but also the underlying utility functions in each health state.

Figure 4.2 illustrates the character of the survey information. Respondents assessed their initial job risk p_1 and their starting wage rate w_1. This yielded point A on the constant expected utility locus EU. After being shown the hazard warning, they assessed the new job risk p_2 and the required wage rate to keep them indifferent to bearing the risk, or w_2, which is point B on the constant expected utility locus. At that wage rate w_2, the market offer curve would be for a job posing a higher risk at point C. Market data could never provide the information to estimate the structure of worker utility functions. This claim may seem controversial to many economists, but it reflects the fact that in market contexts we only observe single points along any individual's utility function.[4]

The experiment consequently yields one equality, which is $EU(A) = EU(B)$. Using this information, one can estimate the utility functions in the good-health state as well as the utility function in the injury state.

For example, with logarithmic utility functions, let

$$U(Y) = u[\log(Y)] \qquad (4.1)$$

---

[4] Some economists have attempted to estimate such utility functions, but doing so requires the imposition of substantial theoretical structure that is shared across individuals.

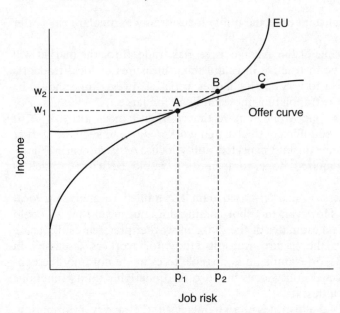

FIG. 4.2 The Market Offer Curve and the Worker's Expected Utility
Function

and

$$V(Y) = v[\log(Y)], \tag{4.2}$$

where u and v are multiplicative parameters. Let t_1 be the income tax
rate when healthy and on the current job, t_2 be the analogous tax rate
for the post-warning job, r_1 be the workers' compensation replacement rate for the healthy state in the current job, and r_2 be the
replacement rate for the post-warning job. The key variable elicited
by the survey is δ, which is the percentage wage increase required
after the warning. The survey equilibrates

$$(1-p_1)u\{\log[Y(1-t_1)]\} + p_1 v\{\log(Yr_1)\} = (1-p_2)u\{\log[Y(1+\delta) \\ (1-t_2)]\} + p_2 v\{\log(Y(1+\delta)r_2)\}. \tag{4.3}$$

Since utility functions are invariant up to a positive linear transfor-
mation, it is not possible to estimate both u and v, but we can estimate their ratio $\alpha = u/v$. After normalizing in this manner, it is

possible to solve the equation above for δ to obtain the nonlinear function that will be estimated.[5]

In the case of the logarithmic utility functions, the value of $U(Y)$ in the healthy state is 1.08 ln Y, and the utility function $V(Y)$ when injured is ln Y. Viscusi and Evans (1990) obtained results reflecting similar characteristics using flexible functional forms, such as first-order and second order Taylor series approximations to general utility functions. These results indicate that $U(Y)$ is greater than $V(Y)$, as one would expect. The more interesting finding pertains to marginal utilities. The results suggest that U' is greater than V' for any given level of income. The higher marginal utility of income when healthy suggests that it would not be optimal to equalize income levels when offered the prospect of efficient actuarially fair insurance. Although it is optimal to equate marginal utilities, the difference in the utility function structures makes it desirable to transfer more income to oneself when healthy than when injured. The underlying rationale is that workers have revealed that they derive greater additional benefit from consumption expenditures when healthy than after disabilities and other injuries.

These results have important consequences for the theory of social insurance. Previous studies either have assumed that $U' > V'$ as the foundation of the model, or have extrapolated the plausibility of such a finding based on the presumed preference when the ill-health fate involves death, in which case $V(Y)$ is the bequest function. These empirical estimates indicate that the marginal utility of income is in fact greater when healthy than after severe injuries.

Explicit information on the shape of utility functions also makes it possible to calculate the optimal value of social insurance. In the case in which there is no insurance loading, this optimal value is 0.85. In the United States, the standard levels of insurance loading for the US workers' compensation system lead to benefits that average $0.80 per

---

[5] More specifically, one obtains

$$\delta = \exp\left\{\frac{K_1 - K_2}{(1-p_2)a + p_2}\right\} - 1 + \epsilon,$$

where

$$K_1 = (1-p_1)\, a \log[Y(1-t_1)] + p_1 \log(Yr_1),$$
$$K_2 = (1-p_2)\, a \log[Y(1-t_2)] + p_2 \log(Yr_2),$$

and ϵ is a random error term. Although somewhat complicated, this expression can be estimated in quite straightforward manner using nonlinear estimation methods.

dollar of premiums. The optimal degree of income replacement for injured workers taking this loading rate into account is 0.68. These estimates exclude the potential influence of moral hazard, which would make the optimal replacement rate less.

Knowledge of the utility functions conveys information on other key economic issues as well. One can determine the income elasticity of the implicit value of injuries, which is 1.10 for the logarithmic utility function estimates and 0.67 assuming a more general Taylor's series approximation to utility functions without imposing an explicit functional form. These estimates provide the basis for extrapolating injury valuation estimates to populations with different income levels and different attitudes toward risk.

A recurring issue in the discussion of the rationality of choice in Chapter 2 pertained to valuations of successive incremental risk changes and increases versus decreases in risk. The logarithmic utility function estimates imply that the willingness-to-accept values for increases in the annual nonfatal injury risk by 0.01 yield an implicit value per injury of $13,401, which is only slightly greater than the $13,286 value for a comparable risk decrease. The predicted gap between willingness-to-pay and willingness-to-accept amounts is not as stark as survey studies of behavior indicate. The high expressed willingness-to-accept values reflect an irrational overreaction to risk increases.

The need to avoid substantial extrapolations in the applicable risk range for compensating differential estimates is also apparent. For a risk increase of 0.915, the implicit value per injury is $20,777, or 1.55 times as great as for a risk increase of 0.01. Compensating differential estimates are pertinent only at the local risk levels for the particular workers at those risks.

COMPENSATING DIFFERENTIAL ESTIMATION

Empirical estimates of compensating differentials relied on a standard wage equation in which the wage rate or the natural logarithm of the wage rate are regressed on the fatality risk and a series of demographic and job characteristic factors X. Thus, economists have estimated equations, such as

$$\ln W = \alpha + \beta_1 Risk + \beta_2' X + \epsilon, \tag{4.4}$$

where β_1 is the coefficient of the death risk variable, β_2 is a vector of coefficients, and ϵ is a random error term. The implicit value of life is simply $\partial W / \partial Risk$, which is simply β_1 in the linear formulation of the model and $\beta_1 Wage$ in the semi-logarithmic version above.

Table 4.2 summarizes most major studies of the value of life using labor market data. Researchers have used a wide variety of data sets to estimate this relationship. For the most part, the general approach has been to obtain a detailed set of data on the worker and the worker's job characteristics and to match to this data set information regarding the job risk based on the worker's industry or occupation. Studies also differ in the extensiveness of the job characteristic variables X, the job risk measure used, and the particular type of worker studied, e.g. blue-collar.

Most studies have focused on typical workers with an average risk given by the fourth column in Table 4.2 of 0.0001. In the case of studies that have focused on higher risk workers, such as that by Thaler and Rosen (1976), the estimated values of life are lower, usually just below $1 million. In contrast, my estimates with more representative workers, such as those in Viscusi (1978*a* and 1979), indicated value-of-life at $4.4 million. These differences reflect the fact that in studies of workers in high-risk jobs there is a different attitude toward risk of those workers who have self-selected themselves into risky occupations. These workers should be most willing to bear substantial job risks, as reflected in their decisions, whereas workers in safer jobs are less willing to incur job hazards.

Studies also differ on other dimensions as well. Some analyses include measures of workers' compensation, which tend to increase the estimated implicit values of life. Some of the results that appear in Table 4.2 are based on models that were intended for a quite different purpose, notably the estimation of implicit rates of time preference with respect to fatality risks. As a result, the studies by Viscusi and Moore (1989) and Moore and Viscusi (1990*a*, 1990*b*) are likely to be less reliable indicators of the risk–money tradeoff than econometric analyses specifically focused on the wage–risk tradeoff.

One particular striking result from the survey of studies in this table is that the evidence for Canada, Japan, Australia, and the United Kingdom is quite similar to that for the United States. Although value-of-life estimates are likely to differ across samples of individuals with different levels of wealth and different preferences, the general orders of magnitude appear to be reasonably consistent.

TABLE 4.2.   Summary of Labor Market Studies of the Value of Life

Author (year)	Sample	Risk variable	Mean risk	Non-fatal risk	Workers' compensation included	Average income level (1990 US$)[a,b]	Implicit value of life ($m)[a]
Smith (1974)	Industry data: Census of manufacturers, US Census, Employment Earnings	Bureau of Labor Statistics (BLS)	NA	Yes	No	22,640	7.2
Thaler and Rosen (1976)	Survey of Economic Opportunity	Society of Actuaries	0.001	No	No	27,034	0.8
Smith (1976)	Current Population Survey (CPS), 1967, 1973	BLS	0.0001	Yes, not signif.	No	NA	4.6
Viscusi (1978a, 1979)	Survey of Working Conditions, 1969–70	BLS, subjective risk of job (SWC)	0.0001	Yes, signif.	No	24,834	4.1
Brown (1980)	National Longitudinal Survey of Young Men 1966–71, 1973	Society of Actuaries	0.002	No	No	NA	1.5
Viscusi (1981)	Panel Study of Income Dynamics, 1976	BLS	0.0001	Yes, signif.	No	17,640	6.5

Study						
Olson (1981)	CPS	BLS	0.0001	Yes, signif.	No	NA	5.2
Marin and Psacharopoulos (1982)	UK Office of Population Censuses and Surveys, 1977	Occupational Mortality, UK	0.0001	No	No	11,287	2.8
Arnould and Nichols (1983)	US Census	Society of Actuaries	0.001	No	Yes	NA	0.9
Butler (1983)	SC Workers' Compensation Data, 1940–69	SC Workers' Compensation Claims Data	0.00005	No	Yes	NA	1.1
Leigh and Folsom (1984)	Panel Study of Income Dynamics, 1974; Quality of Employment Survey, 1977	BLS	0.0001	Yes	No	27,693, 28,734	9.7, 10.3
Smith and Gilbert (1984)	Current Population Survey, 1978	BLS	NA	No	No	NA	0.7
Dillingham (1985)	Quality of Employment Survey, 1977	BLS; constructed by author	0.00008, 0.00014	No	No	20,848	2.5–5.3; 0.9
Leigh (1987)	Quality of Employment Survey, 1977; Current Population Survey, 1977	BLS	NA	No	No	NA	10.4

TABLE 4.2. cont.

Author (year)	Sample	Risk variable	Mean risk	Non fatal risk	Workers' compensation included	Average income level (1990 US$)[a,b]	Implicit value of life ($m)[a]
Herzog and Schlottmann (1990)	US Census, 1970	BLS	NA	No	No	NA	9.1
Moore and Viscusi (1988a)	Panel Study of Income Dynamics, 1982	BLS, NIOSH National Traumatic Occup. Fatality Survey	0.00005, 0.00008	No	Yes	19,444	2.5, 7.3
Moore and Viscusi (1988b)	Quality of Employment Survey, 1977	BLS, discounted expected life years lost; subjective risk of job (QES)	0.00006	No	Yes	24,249	7.3
Garen (1988)	Panel Study of Income Dynamics 1981–2	BLS	NA	Yes	No	NA	13.5
Cousineau, Lacroix, and Girard (1988)	Labor Canada Survey, 1979	Quebec Compensation Board	0.00001	No	No	NA	3.6

Study	Data source	Fatality data / model					
Viscusi and Moore (1989)	Panel Study of Income Dynamics, 1982	NIOSH (National Traumatic Occup. Fatality Survey), Structural Markov Model	0.0001	No	No	19,194	7.8
Moore and Viscusi (1990a)	Panel Study of Income Dynamics, 1982	NIOSH National Traumatic Occup. Fatality Survey, Structural Life Cycle Model	0.0001	No	No	19,194	16.2
Moore and Viscusi (1990b)	Panel Study of Income Dynamics, 1982	NIOSH National Traumatic Occup. Fatality Survey, Structural Integrated Life Cycle Model	0.0001	Yes	Yes	19,194	16.2
Kniesner and Leeth (1991)	Two-digit mfg data, Japan, 1986	Yearbook of Labor Statistics, Japan	0.00003	Yes	No	34,989	7.6
	Two-digit mfg data, Australia, by state, 1984-5	Industrial Accident data, Australia	0.0001	Yes	Yes	18,177	3.3
	Current Population Survey, USA, 1978	NIOSH (National Traumatic Occup. Fatality Survey)	0.0004	Yes	Yes	26,226	0.6

[a] All values are in December 1990 dollars.
[b] NA = Not available.

Economists have also utilized data from decisions outside the labor market to infer an implicit value of life. These studies have explored the values implicit in behavioral responses to risk. Individual choice of highway speed, seatbelt use, smoke detectors, cigarette smoking cessation, and property values also reflect money–risk tradeoffs that have been used as a basis for value-of-life estimates.

The most reliable and extensive studies have involved imputing an implicit value of life from automobile prices. The study by Atkinson and Halvorsen (1990) found that prospective car purchasers valued the greater safety of cars in a manner that reflected implicit value of life of $4.0 million. The analysis by Dreyfus and Viscusi (1995) of used cars went further in that it also considered the durable aspect of car purchases and estimated the purchaser's implicit rate of time preference with respect to safety. We estimated an implicit value of life of $2.9 million–$4.1 million. Perhaps most interesting is that this study also estimated an implied interest rate with respect to risks to life of 10 percent. This value is in a much more reasonable range than economists' estimates of interest rates in contexts such as refrigerator purchases and the energy efficiency of consumer durables.[6] Such studies have estimated discount rates on the order of 30 percent or more with respect to financial savings. Lifetime risk decisions may be less myopic than choices of consumer durables.

Although there is no evidence of uniformity in the estimated value-of-life numbers, some heterogeneity should be expected. The samples differed in terms of their composition, the preferences of the individual, and their opportunities. Since the implicit value of job injuries has an estimated income elasticity of 1.0,[7] it would be quite surprising—indeed, implausible—if all studies estimated similar value-of-life figures. What is clear is that the general order of magnitude of these estimates and the clustering of the estimates around the $3 million–$7 million range suggest a reasonable range of how individuals value risks to their own lives.

As a practical matter, the natural consequence of these findings will not be to pinpoint an explicit value of human life but rather to suggest an appropriate value-of-life range. Until 1983, government agencies did not explicitly value human life because they viewed it as too sacred to monetize. Instead, these agencies calculated what they

---

[6] See e.g. the studies by Hausman (1979) and Gately (1980).
[7] See Viscusi and Evans (1990).

termed 'the cost of death,' which were the medical expenses and the present value of the deceased's lost earnings. In their regulatory analyses, agencies routinely used this cost-of-death figure to value the lives that would be saved through government regulation. In doing so, agencies undervalued human life by roughly a factor of 10 as compared with the proper value-of-life approach.

This practice became the object of a high level policy debate in 1983. The US Occupational Safety and Health Administration and the US Office of Management and Budget disagreed on the merits of the proposed hazard communication regulation, which would have required warnings on all hazardous chemicals used on the job. Using the cost-of-death approach, the regulation failed a benefit–cost test and the US Office of Management and Budget rejected it. After I was called in to resolve this dispute, I prepared an analysis valuing life properly rather than using the cost-of-death approach.[8] Correct valuation of life using willingness-to-pay estimates boosted benefits by about an order of magnitude, a change that was sufficient to make benefits exceed costs.[9] This shift in the economic merits led to approval of the regulation.

It may, of course, be that the value-of-life methodology was not adopted because of its compelling economic foundations. The main attraction to the US Department of Labor and other regulatory agencies is that this methodology boosts estimates of the benefits of government regulation by an order of magnitude above those calculated using the cost of death. Value-of-life estimates make it easier for agencies to justify regulatory efforts. Nevertheless, this policy episode led to the widespread adoption of the correct economic approach to valuing life throughout the US Federal Government. Use of value-of-life figures in benefit assessment does not, however, always lead to recognition of these values in policy decisions, as will be documented below.

Values of life and other risks differ depending on individual preferences. A particularly striking instance of differences in attitudes toward risk is the heterogeneity that individuals display based on other risk-taking activities. Hersch and Viscusi (1990) examined the

[8] My analysis was prepared at the request of then Vice-President Bush to settle the dispute between the two agencies and was generally credited in the US media for settling the controversy. The regulation was approved the day after my analysis reached the White House.

[9] This analysis not only estimated the value of life but also but nonfatal injuries in fatality equivalents.

TABLE 4.3   Implicit Value of a Lost Workday Injury

Equation	Group	Implicit value of a lost workday injury ($ per statistical injury)
1	Full sample	47,900
2	Smokers	26,100
2	Seatbelt users	78,200
2	Nonsmoker–nonseatbelt user	37,800
2	Smoker–seatbelt user	66,400
3	Smoker-nonseatbelt user	26,900
3	Nonsmoker-seatbelt user	83,200
3	Nonsmoker-nonseatbelt user	37,800
3	Smoker–seatbelt user	71,200

Source: Based on Hersch and Viscusi (1990), table 7. The risk variables included are the following (denote the job risk variable by 'Injury'). Equation 1: Injury; equation 2: Injury, Injury × Cigarettes, Injury × Seatbelt use; equation 3: Injury, Injury × Cigarettes, Injury × Seatbelt use, and Injury × Cigarettes × Seatbelt use. 'Cigarettes' is equal to the number of cigarettes smoked by the respondent in an average day.

role of seatbelt use and smoking in affecting wage premiums that workers received on their jobs.[10] As the results in Table 4.3 indicate, the average implicit value of a statistical injury is $47,900 for a representative group of workers. However, smokers display a value of $26,100 and seatbelt users display an implicit value of $78,200. The safety-preferring group of nonsmoker–seatbelt users has an implicit value of injuries of $83,200.

These results highlight the fact that when thinking of the value of life one should not hypothesize that this value is a natural constant such as e or π. Individuals may differ quite starkly in their willingness to bear physical risks. Risk contexts and the character of the risk may affect attitudes toward it as well. Moreover, government policies may wish to provide for varying degrees of protection for different groups. Should we, for example, place a greater weight on a risk that results from involuntary exposures to broadly based environmental risks than on risks that people knowingly choose to bear? People who choose to bear a risk may reveal through this decision a lower value

[10]   For an update with national data, see Hersch and Pickton (1995).

of health status. Risks that result from choice also may have already been compensated through higher wages or lower prices, whereas involuntary risks are not compensated. Protection of people who are exposed to risks involuntarily is not simply a matter of justice with respect to uncompensated hazards. It also may reflect the greater valuations that these unwilling victims of risk may place on their lives.

PUTTING VALUE-OF-LIFE ESTIMATES TO USE[11]

Armed with these empirical estimates of the value of life, how should we deploy them in policy contexts? Suppose that we hear news of a girl trapped in a well or a coal miner trapped underground. Unless we intervene, that person will die. Suppose that the cost of extricating the trapped individual is $10 million, or just outside of the estimated value-of-life range. Should we leave the girl in the well or let the trapped coal miner suffocate? Doing so would certainly be intolerable. In these instances, we are dealing not with statistical lives but rather with identified lives. Even beached whales may lead to rescue efforts that run into the millions of dollars, which is a reflection of society's concern with certain lives.

Situations in which the probability of death can be reduced from 1.0 to 0 are starkly different in that the local rates of risk tradeoff for the individual are appropriate only within narrow risk ranges. Perceived risk changes are greater for certain risk reductions from 1 to 0 for one person than a larger-scale policy involving smaller probabilities of risk reduction that saves one expected statistical life. These biases stem from the character of risk beliefs discussed in relation to Figure 2.3.

Moreover, the estimated value-of-life figures tell us only how we value very small incremental changes in risk. They do not imply that anybody would accept certain death for a fixed amount ranging from $3 million to $7 million. Nor do they suggest that society's broader altruistic concerns should not enter. These amounts may be quite considerable in the case of identified lives.

Our substantial valuation of certain lives is not necessarily inconsistent with more modest valuations of risk for statistical lives.

[11] See Schelling (1968) and Zeckhauser (1975) for thoughtful discussions of the policy issues. Many of the topics below involve altruistic concerns. See Jones-Lee (1991) and Magat and Viscusi (1992).

However, there is the potential for undervaluation of life that might be guarded against by a more thorough thought process regarding society's valuation of risk. In addition to the individual value, how much are we collectively willing to pay to prevent a death? Consider some population of 10,000 people, one of whom may die at random. Suppose our willingness to pay to prevent this random death is less than we would be willing to pay after having learned that the victim of the risk was Arne Ryde. Now suppose that, irrespective of whomever out of the 10,000 individuals is identified after the fact, we would like to revise our willingness to pay value upwards. In that instance, we are probably not exercising enough foresight in our original valuation of the lives that will be lost.

The magnitude of the risk may enter as well. Suppose we must choose between two different policies. One of them saves 10 people out of a village of 100, and the second saves 10 people out of a large city of 1 million. Should we be indifferent between these two policies? Government policies often give priority based on the size of the risk rather than on expected lives at stake. Does this approach have any economic basis?

The underlying economics embodies a number of factors at work. In terms of the potential victim's willingness to pay, the people in the village are buying out of an individual risk of 1/10, whereas the city residents are purchasing a reduction in risk of 1/100,000. Individual willingness to pay for a larger risk reduction will be lower per unit risk because such expenditures are a larger drain on individual resources. More specifically, wealth effects reduce the implicit value per unit risk. For the logarithmic utility function estimates, the implicit value of injuries for a 0.01 reduction in risk is $13,286, and this value drops to $12,865 for a 0.085 reduction in risk.

In terms of society's altruistic valuation, one might conceivably be indifferent since in each case 10 lives will be lost. However, in practice we often target our efforts at the larger risk probability. This may be irrational and may simply affect disproportional media coverage of catastrophes. This pattern of preferences may also indicate that society is uncomfortable with people facing risks that are too great. In this instance, such societal altruistic concerns may run counter to the policy emphasis that would be placed based on individual values. The influence of society's concern with large risks is reflected in regulatory policies that require the rotation of nuclear power plant workers and airplane flight crews to ensure that no particular groups are exposed to too great a risk. However, if the underlying dose–response relationships are linear and pass through the origin, the expected number of deaths will be identical in each case.

Policies that prevent death do not confer immortality. The lives that are saved consequently will differ in duration. From a policy perspective, should one place a greater value on saving the lives of the young rather than the old?

Evidence on individual valuations, with respect to both job risks and automobile safety purchases, suggest that individuals do in fact discount risks to their own well-being. Moreover, the implicit discount rates reflected in these decisions are not inconsistent with observed market rates of interest.[12] Estimates for the discounted value of life exist, making it possible to estimate a quantity-adjusted value of life. However, these estimates do not address many important policy questions. How, for example, do we value years in the lives of children relative to adults? Which years of life matter most? Does the fact that a college student has benefitted from human capital investments and care from parents make this child's life more valuable than it was at birth? Until such problematic issues can be resolved, a useful policy approach is to estimate the cost per life saved as well as the cost per discounted years of life saved to explore the sensitivity of the policy's attractiveness. In practice, the major policy debate is usually not over such minor refinements but about whether risk tradeoffs are being recognized at all.

An equally controversial variation of value-of-life issues is with respect to individual income. It is routine for accident compensation in injury cases to equal the present value of lost earnings, with possible adjustments for consumption and taxes depending on the jurisdiction. With such an approach, the value of compensation after death or after injury will increase proportionally with income. A similar relationship holds for estimates of the implicit value of injuries. The study cited above suggests that the income elasticity of injury valuations is between 0.67 and 1.10.

---

[12] Estimates that yield this result using labor market data are the subjects of studies by Michael Moore and myself; see Viscusi and Moore (1989) and Moore and Viscusi (1990a and 1990b). In addition, as discussed above, Dreyfus and Viscusi (1995) present comparable estimates using price data for used cars. Cropper, Aydede, and Portney (1994) provide evidence on public valuations and their relationship to temporal issues; also see Johannesson and Johansson (1996). Development of the quality-adjusted life year concept first appeared in Zeckhauser and Shepard (1976).

Given such estimates, should we recognize individual heterogeneity or should we treat all lives saved symmetrically? These issues are central to current debates over environmental equity. Based on the beneficiaries' own willingness to pay, there should be differences across population groups. By targeting redistributional efforts to the poor rather than providing risk reduction programs to them that they do not value as much, we will be undertaking efforts that better enhance their own welfare. However, often there is not a policy tradeoff such as this and the poor may not in fact be compensated. One type of implicit income redistribution is to promote risk protection at comparable levels irrespective of the population group.

One should, however, be careful in the quest to equalize protection for all. Policymakers and many risk analysts tend to be relatively affluent. Few readers of this book would consider it an attractive prospect to boost their income by moonlighting on a job that required them to work on a high rise construction project. Indeed, most academics and policymakers would consider the entire blue-collar sector of jobs to be 'too risky.' However, it is not truly a protective measure to eliminate jobs that we consider too risky simply because our greater affluence has given us a different risk–money tradeoff. The appropriate basis for protection is to ask what level of risk workers would choose if they were informed of the risks and could make decisions rationally. This is the level that will result if we properly apply the estimated value-of-life figures, assuming these are accurate.

Distinctions with respect to income also depend on the context in which the distinction is being made. For example, should we regulate airline safety more tightly than highway safety because of the greater affluence of airline passengers? At first blush this practice may be similar to that on the *Titanic* for which there were available lifeboats for only first-class passengers.[13] The difficulty in the case of the *Titanic* is that after the *Titanic* had hit the iceberg the passengers faced the certainty of death, not a lottery. The prospect of certain death is intolerable. Moreover, it is infeasible at that point to ration the available lifeboats.

---

[13] There is, of course, some debate over the accuracy of this characterization of the available lifeboats. However, it is useful for expositional purposes to adopt this simplification. It should be noted there were only 705 survivors out of 2,200 on board, which is generally consistent with inadequate lifeboats scenario that characterizes more popular accounts. For a fuller discussion, see Cahill (1990), especially p. 25.

In contrast, airline safety involves statistical lives. More importantly, requiring airlines to meet a higher level of safety because their passengers are more affluent is not a form of redistribution to the wealthy. The government is not conferring a subsidy. More stringent safety standards will raise the marginal cost of operating airlines, which in turn will raise airline ticket prices that are paid by the passengers themselves. Thus, in market context in which it is the individuals benefitting from the risk reduction who will directly pay for the risk reduction benefits, making distinctions based on affluence appear to be well-founded and less controversial. In contrast, if the policy approach is to use broadly based societal resources to confer risk reduction benefit, the case for making distinctions across income groups becomes much more problematic.

Income differences also impinge on how we treat risks in different countries. Some advocates of protective measures have urged that the advanced countries do not import goods produced in a hazardous manner. These policy advocates often make speeches proclaiming that we should protect the exploited workers of Thailand, Indonesia, or other less developed countries by refusing to import goods that are produced without observing our labor safety standards.

However, this kind of protection will in fact decrease their welfare by lowering their income. Moreover, such protective measures ignore differences in the countries' stages of development. Requiring less developed countries to meet the same safety standards that now prevail in the United States and Western Europe makes no more sense than it would have for us to have met such stringent safety standards in the early part of the twentieth century. Increases in individual income and wealth are a powerful force for promoting individual health, as we will explore in Chapter 5. Policy measures that foster increased economic development ultimately will improve the well-being of these less developed countries. Not only will the workers benefit directly by having more income to purchase medical care, food, and other necessities, but as a result of increased income they will increasingly demand the kind of risk and environmental protections that are the norm in the developed nations.

An analogous type of policy is the concern with whether the same standards should be applied to risky exports as are imposed within a country. Unless there are going to be misperceptions abroad regarding the quality levels provided, policies that permit companies to market goods that are consistent with the risk standards in the purchasing countries appear to be more sensible than those that seek to impose a uniform risk requirement universally.

This is more than an abstract issue. US pharmaceutical firms are unable to produce in the United States pharmaceutical products that have not yet been approved by the US Food and Drug Administration.[14] This requirement often stifles the international competitiveness of US firms, since the drug approval process in Western Europe is much more rapid than in the United States, where companies often face inordinate delays. As a result of this policy, US companies have been forced to move their production operations overseas in order to circumvent the regulatory requirement. The export requirement consequently imposes needless inefficiencies in this instance.

A possible counterexample might be the side gas tanks on General Motors trucks, which can catch fire upon impact. Once this product defect has become apparent, should American companies be permitted to unload the defective trucks on foreign markets for which there are no comparable safety regulations? If the defect of the product is properly identified and can be understood by the users, it might be reasonable to permit such marketing, particularly if the trucks might be safer than the vehicles currently operated in these countries. However, in all likelihood proper characterization of the fire risk, which is quite vivid and dramatic, would discourage purchase and prompt regulation in a wide variety of countries.

Differences in income levels also serve as a policy concern with respect to temporal variations in risk regulation. To what degree should we protect future generations as opposed to providing for current consumption? Effective actions to reduce the current trajectory toward climate change and global warming will, for example, entail significant sacrifices in terms of current economic growth. What kinds of sacrifice are warranted? Future generations will probably be more affluent than we are except under the most dire economic forecasts. Just as we prefer a safer and cleaner environment than did our ancestors, future generations will place a higher value on environmental amenities than will the less affluent current generation. Is it rational for us to sacrifice more now to provide the kind

---

[14] This longstanding regulation was being considered for elimination in 1996.

of environment that future generations would prefer if they could compensate us in an intergenerational bargain?

Such bargains have a seemingly perverse income redistribution effect. Current generations are poorer, and the above approach would in effect ask them to sacrifice to provide for more affluent future populations. On a retrospective basis, it would seem unreasonable to have required earlier generations lacking indoor plumbing and electricity to make significant sacrifices to improve our well-being. It is conceivable that sacrifices by the current generation will appear equally inequitable in retrospect, centuries from now.

The economic efficiency approach would be to leave future generations with an efficient level of environmental quality. In particular, what conditions would we contract for if we could carry out a bargain with future generations? This efficiency bargain reference point is only a thought experiment, but it may nevertheless provide a useful guide toward an appropriate level of environmental protection.

The reality, however, is that current generations are not compensated. As a result, they may be unwilling to follow this efficiency reference point. Within the context of this discussion, it is noteworthy that in this instance recognition of heterogeneity of valuations resulting from income differences will lead to tougher environmental standards than we would have adopted had the greater valuations of future generations been ignored.

THE POLICY CHALLENGE

Valuing life has now become a routine part of policy analyses. Moreover, economists have not stopped with lives. Studies have estimates the value of a wide range of other health outcomes, such as cancer.[15]

These values could be a key building block in policy decisions. For example, the four key components might be the number of lives at risk, the probability of death, the value of life, and the cost of eliminating the risk. Unfortunately, it is typically the probability of death alone that triggers policy intervention. Thus, the role of the preferences of the people who are to be protected by the regulation usually

---

[15] My past studies, including survey analyses, have valued nonfatal job injuries, fatal cancer, nonfatal cancer, chronic bronchitis, multiple sclerosis, peripheral neuropathy, poisonings, and other health effects.

do not enter as a matter of policy concern even though they do affect the background policy analyses. Ignoring individual preferences would pose substantial problems for the soundness of personal decisions. As subsequent chapters document, it would also create difficulties for government policy.

5
Risk–Risk Analysis

RISK–RISK TRADEOFFS

Government policymakers often do not have the discretion to select policies based on their overall costs and benefits, where these benefits are assessed using implicit values of life. There may, for example, be legislative constraints that require a regulatory agency to eliminate certain kinds of risks or decrease them to a particular level. From a political standpoint, the fiction that there is no compromising safety in an effort to conserve expenditures often drives actual policy choices.

These myopically specified policy objectives may, however, divert resources from more beneficial lifesaving efforts and may even create counterproductive effects. Indeed, these adverse consequences may include risk repercussions of policies that offset the direct risk effects the policies might have. The concern in this chapter will be with risk–risk tradeoffs, how they arise, and how policymakers can better recognize their role in formulating risk policies.

We will distinguish two principal risk–risk effects. The first type of risk–risk tradeoff is that there may be competing risks of a particular type arising either from the policy itself or from behavioral responses to it. Banning artificial sweeteners because of their potential carcinogenicity may lead to the use of substitute sweeteners that also adversely affect on health or to increase the intake of sugar, with its associated effect on obesity and heart disease. Chlorination of drinking water reduces the risk from contaminated water but creates a potential cancer hazard; on balance, the health risk is lower after chlorination. Recalls of motor vehicles for needed repairs require that the drivers bring the vehicle back to the dealership for these repairs, and in so doing some drivers may be injured or killed. Lowering speed limits on major highways decreases average driving speed but increases its variance and the incentive to drive on back roads, each of which has an adverse effect on safety. A particularly dramatic example is the requirement by the US Consumer Product Safety Commission that children's sleepwear be coated with the flam retardant Tris; this reduced the risk of flammability, but created a new risk since Tris was found to be carcinogenic.

A second variant of risk–risk analysis may be less obvious. Regulatory efforts entail regulatory costs, diverting society's resources from other uses. Higher prices, lower wages, and higher taxes that result from regulation represent real opportunity costs to society. To the extent that these funds could have been expended on a market basket of goods including health-regulated components such as medical care, there will be an adverse health effect. The main controversy is how substantial these effects are and how ineffective regulatory expenditures must be for these regulations to have a counterproductive influence. It is on these issues that we focus in this chapter.

BEHAVIORAL RESPONSES TO REGULATION

Regulatory analyses frequently take an engineering approach. Assuming no changes in individual behavior, the regulation sets out to change aspects of the safety technology, which in turn will produce the desired safety improvements.

Unfortunately, this scenario leaves out the intervening linkage of behavioral responses to regulations. A well known example of such a response is the influence of automobile seatbelts, which was first explored in detail by Peltzman (1975). Since seatbelts reduce the risk of injury to the driver associated with driving fast, the effect will be to make driving faster more desirable in order to reduce travel time. As a result, the increased driving speed will dampen and possibly offset the safety benefits associated with the introduction of seatbelts. The intuition behind this result is reflected in a somewhat different example. For much the same reason that few would question that it is more rational to drive more slowly on icy streets than on dry ones, there is an incentive to drive more slowly in a world in which there are no seatbelts.

The empirical magnitude of this effect remains a matter of considerable dispute.[1] There does, however, seem to be a general

---

[1] For a review of this evidence and additional perspectives, see Blomquist (1988, 1991), Crandall *et al.* (1986), and Adams (1995).

consensus that there is at least some muting of the effectiveness that seatbelts would have had because of the increased risk of injury to motorcyclists and pedestrians resulting from faster driving.

A particularly dramatic example of a behavioral response to regulation that I identified is the effect of safety caps on potentially poisonous products. Child poisonings from household consumer products were a leading cause of injury and death among preschool children. As a result, the government mandated a variety of safety cap requirements on hazardous products.

To explore the efficiency of these safety caps, I first compiled the overview statistics in Table 5.1. After the introduction of safety caps in the United States, the percentage of aspirin sold with safety caps was just over 50 percent. Poisoning from safety cap bottles was substantial, rising from 40 percent in 1972 to 73 percent by 1978. Much of the reason for these poisonings is that parents left the caps off the bottles altogether. The share of poisonings from open bottles rose from 41 percent in 1972 to 49 percent in 1978. Problems also arose from apparent misperception of the efficacy of the caps. Because safety caps were often referred to even by prominent Consumer Product Safety Commission officials as being 'childproof' caps, parents may have been lulled into a false sense of security. As a result, after the advent of safety caps, there was a rash of poisonings from similar products that at the time did not have caps. These increases were apparent in regression analyses that controlled for the poisoning trend.

Figure 5.1 illustrates the nature of the mechanisms. Suppose that the expected loss to the consumers of safety-related effort is given by the curve EL_0. Facing these prospects, the consumer makes a decision with regard to the optimal amount of safety effort, which in this case is A. After the advent of safety caps, the expected loss associated with any degree of safety-related effort diminishes with the new expected loss curve given by EL_1. If the consumer were to adopt the same level of safety precautions and take point B, the expected loss would be reduced by the vertical distance between A and B. Because of the increased safety provided by the caps, there will be an incentive for consumers to dampen their precaution level. If they select point C, then the expected loss will be the same as it was before the advent of the caps. If they were to select point F, their expected loss would be greater. It is potentially feasible for consumers to select

TABLE 5.1   Poisoning Incidence since the Introduction of Safety Caps on Aspirins and Analgesics

	1971	1972	1973	1974	1975	1976	1977	1978
Aspirin								
Sold with safety caps (%)	—	53	56	56	59	56	55	52
Poisonings from safety-capped bottles (%)	—	40	52	60	59	67	71	73
Share of poisonings due to open bottles (%)	—	41	43	44	48	46	44	49
Aspirin and analgesics								
Poisonings from safety-capped bottles (%)	—	34	44	53	54	63	67	66
Share of poisonings due to open bottles (%)	—	43	43	44	47	44	39	47
Total poisonings	168,930	167,270	153,670	126,520	137,010	112,860	112,840	111,420

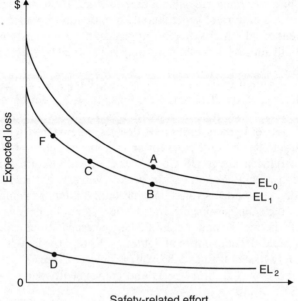

FIG. 5.1 Safety Mechanisms and the Choice of Precautions

point *F*, though this outcome is not likely because the conditions for it to occur are quite stringent.[2]

The greater danger is that consumers will misperceive the effect of the safety device on the safety effort–loss tradeoff. If the actual loss–safety effort frontier is EL_1, but consumers believe it is EL_2, then they may select a point such as *D*. In that instance, not only will their safety-related effort diminish, but they will perceive that there is relatively small expected loss whereas in fact the true expected loss is given by that at point *F*.

Regression analysis of poisoning trends indicates that there has been no statistically significant influence of safety caps on the trend in poisonings from regulated commodities, such as prescription drugs, various categories of aspirin, turpentine, or solvents and thinners.[3] However, after the advent of such regulations, there has been a surge in product-related poisonings for unregulated internal medicines, analgesics (e.g. acetaminophen products), psychopharmacological

[2] See Chapter 13 of Viscusi (1992).   [3] See Viscusi (1985).

agents, hormones and miscellaneous medicines. These results are consistent with a pattern of general laxity of parental responsibility after the advent of safety caps. Parents appear to have assumed that safety caps would address the child poisoning risks posed by such medicines and products.

To better identify the mechanisms underlying such effects, I have undertaken a study of parental response to safety devices for cigarette lighters.[4] Respondents rated the risks of conventional lighters and the risks of lighters with safety devices, where these lighters were given to smokers in three cities for an in-home placement before they were introduced under US Consumer Product Safety Commission regulations. On a ten point scale, with 0 being no risk and 10 being very risky, respondents rated conventional lighters as being 8.25 in terms of their dangerousness and the new safety lighters as 4.10. In terms of whether the parents should be concerned about child safety, parents rated the conventional lighter as 9.3 and the lighter with the child safety mechanism as 5.85. Safety devices decrease risk assessments and expected injury costs and consequently should dampen safety precautions.

Using the results of the in-house placement component in conjunction with the efficacy of the safety mechanism in reducing injuries, it is possible to calculate the extent of the safety improvement that will be muted by the behavioral response because of the increased perception of safety. The estimates of the risk offset or 'moral hazard' effects varied depending on the survey evidence that was used. Using information on whether parents intended to take precautions with respect to the lighters, the moral hazard effects were 43 percent of the total change in the probability of injury. Based on respondents' statements with respect to whether they would grant children access to the lighters, the empirical assessment is that 75 percent of the safety improvement would be negated by the moral hazard response. These estimates consequently suggest that from just under half to possibly up to three-fourths of the safety gains that result from the improved safety properties of lighters with safety mechanisms would be offset by the behavioral response.

The general lesson here is not that technological safety improvements are necessarily ill-conceived or should not be pursued by the government; rather, in promulgating such regulations, there should

---

[4] See Viscusi and Cavallo (1994).

be cognizance of the role of behavioral responses that may mute the beneficial effects that regulations would have. Moreover, people may misperceive the efficacy of the safety mechanism by believing that they make products risk-free. Governmental informational efforts can play a constructive role by altering consumers to the risk and to the continuing need for vigilance with respect to safety.

REGULATORY EXPENDITURE AND THE WEALTH–RISK RELATIONSHIP

Regulatory expenditures necessarily decrease the resources available for other uses. Because of regulations, consumers pay higher prices, workers receive lower wages, and the public at large pays higher taxes. Regulatory costs represent a real opportunity cost of resources that could have been allocated elsewhere.

Two types of regulatory cost effect are pertinent. First, because regulations stimulate economic activity to comply with the regulations, there will be people who will be injured or killed as part of this compliance effort. Second, because of the wealth–risk relationship there will be a second influence on safety as well. Regulatory costs, in effect, make society poorer in other ways. Since economic progress has been the principal contributor to our improved health and well-being, wasteful regulatory expenditures may involve real health costs.

Consider first the injury costs associated with regulatory expenditures. Using an input–output model, Richard Zeckhauser and I estimated the injury cost of output as a fraction of the value of total output for a wide variety of industry groups.[5] For example, suppose that regulation results in construction activity, such as the removal of hazardous waste, or miscellaneous manufacturing activity, such as the production of pollution control devices. In terms of the nonfatal injury costs, construction activities generate injuries that, when valued at $50,000 per injury, comprise 3 percent of total output. Manufacturing activities also generate injury costs that are 3 percent of total output. Fatality costs are a smaller percentage of output. The fatality costs of output, which we calculated using a value of $5 million per fatality, are under 1 percent—0.7 percent for construction

[5] See Viscusi and Zeckhauser (1994).

and 0.3 percent for manufacturing. The total injury and fatality costs of output consequently are 3–4 percent of all output costs. Put somewhat differently, every time government regulations require $100 of economic activity to comply with the regulation, there is an injury and fatality cost of $3–$4. Suppose that regulations are particularly ineffective and generate risk reduction costs that comprise only 2 percent of regulatory costs. Such regulations will actually be counterproductive in terms of their risk effects.

A second type of counterproductive influence is that there is an adverse risk effect of regulatory policies because of the decrease in available resources resulting from regulatory expenditures. Such allocations decrease other spending for improvements in health status. There is both a direct reduction in mortality-reducing expenditures, such as health care, and diminished expenditures for higher quality consumer items, such as safer cars, which have a positive income elasticity of demand. This class of influences can be traced to the fact that being richer is healthier, an effect I first documented with respect to job safety choices by income group.[6]

A number of studies have attempted to estimate the income–mortality relationship directly by regressing mortality rates on various measures, including income. How much must total income drop for there to be an expected fatality occurring because society is poorer? Various studies have used international data, information pertaining to retirement behavior, and evidence regarding changing economic conditions such as recessions to estimate this relationship. These direct estimates yield income losses that lead to a statistical death ranging from $1.9 million to $33.2 million (November 1992 dollars).[7]

The two-directional cuasality between income status and mortality complicates such investigations. Good health increases one's earnings capabilities, creating a joint relationship between measures of health status and income. Disentangling these effects has remained a continuing problem.

There is an additional difficulty with some of these studies in terms of the plausibility of the results. Some studies have found that the estimated income loss amount that leads to the loss of a statistical life is similar to the implicit value of saving a statistical life, which we found in Chapter 4 to average about $5 million. Such low cost

---

[6] See Viscusi (1978*b*) for examination of these issues.
[7] For a review of these studies, see Viscusi (1994*b*).

amounts for generating a statistical death do not make sense economically. For such offset levels to be observed, the average life-saving decisions reflected in money–risk tradeoffs must be counterproductive and on balance lead to a net increase in mortality rather than a reduction in mortality. If the $5 million value for saving a statistical life were a correct estimate, then it would not be rational to have an expenditure cutoff figure that leads to the loss of a statistical life below that amount. Otherwise, people would be spending money to save lives in a way that leads to safety effects that on balance are counterproductive. Safety expenditures, on balance, would be counterproductive.

THE VALUE OF LIFE LINKAGE: THEORY

To exploit this potential linkage between the implicit value of saving a statistical life and the income level that leads to the loss of a statistical life, I developed a theoretical model to capture this interrelationship.[8] Consider first the individual choice process. The worker selects the safety level s offered by the firm in which he or she works. The individual also picks a level of own health investment h. These two choice variables govern the worker's probability of survival $q(s,h)$, where $q_s > 0$, $q_h > 0$, $q_{ss} < 0$, $q_{hh} < 0$, and $q_{sh} \le 0$. The worker's probability of death, which has been the focal point of the discussion thus far, is simply $1 - q(s,h)$.

Following the standard compensating differential reasoning, the market equilibrium wage schedule will provide for compensating differentials for risk. As a result, we will assume that $w_s < 0$, and $w_{ss} \le 0$. Let A denote the worker's other income. Worker consumption is consequently $A + w(s) - h$. Health investments do not provide utility directly but are worthwhile since they increase the probability of survival.

For the two states of the world, the worker's preferences are characterized by $U(A + w(s) - h)$ if the worker survives and a bequest function $V(A + w(s) - h)$ if he or she does not. The worker would rather be alive than not, is not risk-loving, and for any given level of income has a higher marginal utility of income when alive: $U(X) > V(X)$, $U_X > V_X > 0$, and $U_{XX}, V_{XX} \le 0$.

[8] See Viscusi (1994*a*) for fuller development of alternative models.

The worker's decision is to

$$\text{Max}_{s,h} \ EU = q(s,h) \ U(A + w(s) - h) + (1 - q(s,h)) \ V(A + w(s) - h).$$
(5.1)

The choice with respect to h leads to the first-order condition

$$\frac{1}{q_h} = \frac{U - V}{qU' + (1 - q)V'},$$
(5.2)

and the choice of s yields

$$\frac{-w_s}{q_s} = \frac{U - V}{qU' + (1 - q)V'}.$$
(5.3)

The joint implication of these conditions is that

$$\frac{1}{q_h} = \frac{-w_s}{q_s} = \frac{U - V}{qU' + (1 - q)V'}.$$
(5.4)

The commonality of these linkages in the two choices is not accidental. The first term—$1/q_h$—is the inverse of the change in mortality with respect to health investments, which is simply the marginal value of life for health investments. Similarly, the second term is the marginal value of life reflected by the worker's job choice, or what we simply referred to in Chapter 4 as the value of life. The marginal value of life is the same for both classes of choice. If it differed, the person could achieve greater safety gains for the same cost by reallocating across the health care—job safety choices. For example, the worker could take a safer job for lower pay. The final term in equation (5.4) is the utility change associated with the accident normalized by the expected marginal utility of income. This expression first appeared in Viscusi (1979) and represents the pivotal utility term in the compensating differential literature.

To understand the meaning of this final term, it is useful to rewrite (5.4) in words:

$$\begin{aligned}\textit{Marginal value} \quad &\textit{Marginal value} \\ \textit{of life for} \quad &= \textit{of life for} \\ \textit{health investments} \quad &\textit{job risks}\end{aligned}$$

$$= \frac{\textit{Utility change with ill health}}{\textit{Expected marginal utility of income}}. \quad (5.5)$$

A possibly more instructive rewriting of this equation is

$$\frac{\text{Utility change}}{\text{with ill health}} = \frac{\text{Marginal value}}{\text{of life for}} \times \frac{\text{Expected marginal}}{\text{utility of income}} .$$
$$\text{health investments}$$

$$= \frac{\text{Marginal value}}{\text{of life for}} \times \frac{\text{Expected marginal}}{\text{utility of income}} .$$
$$\text{job risks} \qquad (5.6)$$

In each case, the value of life multiplied by the expected marginal utility of income equals the decline in utility resulting from death.

In addressing the role of government regulations, let us focus on the narrow issue of whether they decrease risk. Even if the regulations do not produce benefits commensurate with their costs, at the very minimum they should at least decrease risk levels, or equivalently increase the probability of survival. Regulations will have three effects. First, they will increase job safety directly, where for concreteness we focus on the job safety context. Second, because of the greater job safety levels, workers will have less of an incentive to invest in personal health expenditures.[9] Finally, regulatory costs decrease workers' income A. Combining these effects, regulation will have a positive effect on the survival probability if

$$\Delta q = \frac{\partial q}{\partial s} \Delta s + \frac{\partial q}{\partial h} \frac{\partial h}{\partial s} \Delta s + \frac{\partial q}{\partial h} \frac{\partial h}{\partial A} \Delta A > 0. \qquad (5.7)$$

The policy implications of this condition take on a somewhat different form upon rearranging the terms, or

$$\frac{-\Delta A}{\left(\frac{\partial q}{\partial s} + \frac{\partial q}{\partial h} \frac{\partial h}{\partial s} \right) \Delta s} < \frac{1}{\frac{\partial q}{\partial h} \frac{\partial h}{\partial A}} . \qquad (5.8)$$

The term on the left side of (5.8) is the average cost per life saved, i.e. the regulatory costs divided by the increased mortality. The term on the right side of (5.8) is the value of life for health care investments—$(1/\partial q/\partial h)$—divided by the marginal propensity to spend on health out of income—$\partial h/\partial A$. Regulation will have a beneficial effect on safety provided that the

$$\frac{\text{Average cost per}}{\text{life saved}} < \frac{\text{Marginal value of life}}{\text{Marginal propensity spent on health}} . \qquad (5.9)$$

---

[9] This result, which appears in Viscusi (1994*a*), is based on the regulatory analog of the individual choice model above. The level of s is constrained through regulation.

Inequality (5.9) consequently establishes the linkage between the regulatory expenditure that leads to the loss of a statistical life and the more traditional value of life.

THE VALUE OF LIFE LINKAGE:
EMPIRICAL EVIDENCE

If people spent the entirety of the marginal dollar on health, any government program that saved lives at a cost more than the value of life reflected in private health care expenditures would be counterproductive and would increase risk. Thus, any policy that failed a benefit–cost test would also fail a risk–risk test. Since people do not spend all their income on mortality-reducing expenditures (i.e. the marginal propensity to spend on health is less than 1), the level of regulatory expenditures per statistical life saved that will be counterproductive will exceed the value of life reflected in individual decisions.

To assess the extent of this difference, we need estimates of a key parameter—how much of each additional dollar would go toward mortality-reducing expenditures. For empirical purposes, let us treat health expenditures as the principal allocations related to mortality.[10]

Evidence for the United States indicates that marginal propensity to spend on health care out of income ($\partial h / \partial A$) ranges from 0.09 to 0.12. Table 5.2 presents similar evidence based on OECD data based on a regression of the log of per capita health expenditures against the gross domestic product per capita, the unemployment rate, and in some cases a series of other variables, such as dummy variables for the year and country. The estimates of the marginal propensity to spend on health out of income are reasonably stable and range from 0.08 to 0.09.

The implication of both US and international data is consequently that there is a marginal propensity to spend on health care of about 10 percent. In conjunction with equation (5.9), this result implies that the regulatory expenditure that leads to the loss of a statistical life is approximately ten times greater than the value that people are willing to pay per statistical life to save lives. This result is also consistent

[10] In Lutter, Morrall, and Viscusi (1996), we generalize this analysis to capture other health-related expenditures that have an adverse effect, such as excessive drinking, choice of one's diet, and cigarette smoking.

TABLE 5.2. Log Per Capita Health Expenditure Weighted Least-Squares Regressions with OECD Data, 1960–1989

Independent variables	1	2	3	4	5	6
Intercept	-4.432 (0.043)	-4.353 (0.049)	-3.552 (0.106)	-4.586 (0.550)	-4.522 (0.065)	-3.739 (0.292)
Ln (gross domestic product per capita)	1.207 (0.005)	1.196 (0.007)	1.091 (0.017)	1.224 (0.007)	1.221 (0.009)	1.114 (0.044)
Ln (unemployment) rate)	—	0.008 (0.011)	-0.006 (0.008)	—	-0.022 (0.013)	0.002 (0.009)
Other variables included; comments	—	—	29 year dummy variables, 23 country dummy variables	Purchasing power parity	Purchasing power parity	Purchasing power parity, 29 year dummy variables, 23 country dummy variables
$\bar{R}^2$	0.987	0.986	0.998	0.980	0.978	0.997
Sample size	675	589	589	671	585	585
$\partial h/\partial A$	0.089	0.089	0.081	0.089	0.089	0.081

with one's economic intuition, which is that the regulatory expenditure that would be counterproductive and would lead to the loss of a statistical life is necessarily greater than the value people are willing to pay to save a statistical life.

TABLE 5.3.   Health Effects of Regulatory Expenditures

	$100bn in regulatory costs
Direct risk effects	
Value of lives and injuries resulting from direct production risk	$4.1bn
Mortality–income effects of regulatory costs	
Lives lost	2,000
Value of lives lost (at $5m per life)	$10bn
Policy tests	
Total health risk costs	$14.1bn
Health risk costs as % of total costs	14%
Critical cost-per-life threshold for beneficial health effects	$35.7m

Table 5.3 summarizes the combined influence of the direct mortality costs of regulatory expenditures and the effect that is operative through the income–mortality relationship. Consider the effect of $100 billion in regulatory costs. The direct production risk cost of these expenditures if $4.1 billion. Because these expenditures divert resources from allocations such as health care, there will be 2,000 lives lost with a total value of $10 billion. The total health risk cost is therefore $14.1 billion. The cost of the direct health risks and the mortality–income-related health risk costs consequently are 14 percent of total regulatory expenditures. If regulatory costs fail to generate risk reduction benefits that comprise at least 14 percent of the total regulatory expenditure, the net risk effect on society will be adverse.

In terms of a critical value of life, regulations that save lives at a cost of $35.7 million per statistical life saved on balance will have a counterproductive effect on total societal mortality. Although this calculation was made for expenditures with respect to construction-related costs, it is similarly feasible to estimate such figures for manufacturing expenditures and other regulatory efforts.

CONCLUSION

Risk–risk analysis is not a first-best approach to policy analysis. Ideally, one would want to pursue policies that on balance generate benefits in excess of their costs. The existence of a mortality–regulatory expenditure relationship does require that conventional benefit–cost criteria be modified,[11] but the extent of such a modification is not great.

The more practical importance of risk–risk analysis is as an imperfect substitute for benefit–cost analysis in situations in which benefit–cost analysis is not permitted or is not being pursued for some political reason. Policymakers may, for example, be unwilling to put an implicit dollar value on a statistical life. Their enabling legislation may, for example, require them to pursue a policy of risk reduction irrespective of costs. The danger of such efforts is that if they are highly ineffective the net effect of such policies will be adverse. Indeed, as the calculations presented here for construction-related policies suggest, expenditure levels above $35.7 million per statistical life saved will in fact be harmful to society in terms of their risk consequences.

Consider the consequences of an extreme hypothetical situation. Suppose that the policy has no beneficial effects whatsoever on risk. The effort simply entailed nothing more productive than getting workers to dig ditches and fill them back up again. These activities would have no beneficial effects on safety, yet injuries could occur in the course of such efforts. Although regulatory policies seldom approach this extreme in terms of their lack of efficacy, in some instances the risks being targeted are so negligible, and the risk effects are so small, that the adverse effects on society outweigh the potential risk reduction benefits. In these cases, one should be cognizant that wasteful regulatory expenditures, even with the laudatory objective of promoting individual health, may make society worse off even if health is our sole concern.

[11] See Viscusi (1994*a*) for fuller details.

6

Risk Analysis and Regulatory Policy

Risk regulations must be selective. The presence of health and safety risks is ubiquitous. It is simply not feasible to eliminate all risks that we face and to ensure zero risk outcome.

Consider, for example, the following risks that increase the annual risk of death by 1/1,000,000.[1] Among the risk exposures that pose a 1/1,000,000 fatality risk are living two days in New York or Boston (air pollution), travelling ten miles by bicycle (accident), eating 40 tablespoons of peanut butter (liver cancer caused by aflatoxin B), living for 150 years within 20 miles of a nuclear power plant (cancer caused by radiation), and one chest X-ray taken in a good hospital (cancer caused by radiation).

Even items in our diet that we consider to be completely safe may in fact pose some minor cancer risk because of the presence of natural carcinogens.[2] Fruits and vegetables often contain chemicals that are potentially carcinogenic since these chemicals serve a constructive function as a form of protection against insects and other threats. Among the many dietary items that are potential carcinogens are wine, beer, lettuce, apples, mushrooms, pears, orange juice, coffee, plums, peanut butter, celery, carrots, potatoes, bacon, and parsley. In each case natural carcinogens contribute to the presence of the risk. In some cases, these natural carcinogens are more potent causes of cancer than are many regulated risk exposures. For example, US environmental regulations eliminated the use of Alar as a pesticide for apples. But although a six ounce glass of apple juice does pose a cancer risk, the risk is no greater than that posed by the natural carcinogens in two slices of bread or the natural carcinogens

---

[1] The data discussed below are from Wilson (1979).
[2] See Gold *et al.* (1992).

in one mushroom, one whole carrot, or a piece of any of a wide variety of fruits, including apples.[3]

Clearly, some distinctions are needed. We need to identify which risks are important and which are not. Moreover, we have to assess how costly it is to alter the risk so that we can focus our risk reduction efforts on the risks that we can eliminate most cheaply. Risks from automobile travel are considerable, but we will be reluctant to make cars as safe as tanks because doing so would impose considerable direct expense and fuel efficiency costs.

Some regulatory policies do attempt to distinguish the risk magnitude. However, the way in which this is done may mirror inadequacies in individual decisions. One anomaly in people's responses to risk is that they often overreact to newly discovered risks compared with familiar risks. US federal regulatory policies for pharmaceutical products and medical devices are subject to similar biases.

There are two potential errors in a regulatory approval process for products such as drugs. A type I error involves rejecting a drug that is safe and effective; a type II error involves approving a drug that is not safe and effective. Current government policies place excessive weight on type II errors in an effort to avoid problems such as that posed by Thalidomide. This drug led to birth defects in the United Kingdom but was never approved for use in the United States. Regulatory officials at the US Food and Drug Administration (FDA) are very sensitive to the risk of approving a drug that could turn out to be the next Thalidomide. In contrast, there is comparatively little penalty for delaying the entry of new drugs in the market. As a result, new drug approvals in the United States often lag behind those in Western Europe even though the United States leads in research. The bureaucratic incentives are much more sensitive to errors of commission than errors of omission. People who cause undesirable outcomes by *acting* receive more blame than people who cause undesirable outcomes by *not* acting. The victims of a faulty drug that has been approved will be identifiable individuals. In contrast, heart patients who could have profited from drugs that should have been approved but were not because of the undue emphasis on avoiding type II errors will entail a loss of statistical lives rather than identified lives. Government policymakers are much more

---

[3] One possible rationale for regulating Alar is that young children who drink apple juice are a highly exposed group and potentially also more sensitive to the risk exposure.

responsive to well identified constituencies than to broadly based groups whose statistical lives will be jeopardized because of the failure of government policy.

It is noteworthy in this regard that the most expedited approval process for prescription drugs in the United States has been for AIDS drugs. Because the AIDS lobby is a well identified group that is at high risk and politically well organized, it has been successful in pressuring the Food and Drug Administration (FDA) to put drugs targeted toward AIDS on a more expedited approval process. For decades the FDA has espoused support of more rapid approval for drugs targeted at life-threatening diseases, and has claimed success in expediting approvals. However, the degree of progress is overstated because there has been a change in the calculation of the approval lag time. The clock is now restarted whenever the FDA requests additional information on a drug. The result is that, notwithstanding claims of faster approval, drugs other than AIDS-related ones continue to languish in the US drug approval process.

The bias in terms of the focus of risk policy is also exemplified in the attitude toward synthetic chemicals. Natural chemicals pose familiar risks to which society has become relatively accustomed. In contrast, synthetic chemicals involve new hazards that pose risks to which people have not been accustomed. In much the same way that people tend to overreact to changes in the accustomed level of risks, in particular increases in new kinds of risk there is a similar reaction on the part of government agencies.

Consider the statistics in Table 6.1, which are based on a large sample of 365 chemicals. The results in this table parallel more formal regression analyses. Reported tests of statistical significance pertain to differences in means across the columns. Panel (*a*) gives a profile of the chemicals' properties depending on whether animal tests using rats showed that the chemical was carcinogenic. Overall, 181 of the chemicals were found to be carcinogenic and 184 were not. As the results indicated, there is no statistically significant difference between chemicals that have been found to be carcinogenic and those that have not with respect to either their synthetic character or their overall frequency of regulation. Some types of regulation do, however, affect carcinogenic and non-carcinogenic chemicals differently. Somewhat surprisingly, FDA regulations are more likely to regulate chemicals not found to be carcinogenic. Multiple regression analysis reported in Viscusi and Hakes (1997) indicates that this result is due

Risk Analysis and Regulatory Policy 87

TABLE 6.1.   Risk Character and Regulatory Policies for Chemicals in Sample[a]

(a) Chemical profile based on whether there is evidence of carcinogenicity

	Carcinogenic $n=181$	Not carcinogenic $n=184$
Synthetic chemical (0–1)	0.740 (0.440)	0.723 (0.449)
Regulated chemical (0–1)	0.669 (0.472)	0.587 (0.494)
FDA regulation (0–1) (n= 86,107)	0.372 (0.486)	0.449 (0.500)
EPA regulation (0–1)	0.586*** (0.494)	0.435*** (0.497)
OSHA regulation (0–1)	0.282** (0.451)	0.169*** (0.375)

(b) Chemical profile based on synthetic character of the chemical

	Synthetic chemical $n=267$	Natural chemical $n=98$
Not carcinogenic (0–1)	0.498 (0.501)	0.520 (0.502)
Rats' TD_{50} test level	323.1 (842.9)	302.4 (1327.5)
Regulated (0–1)	0.640 (0.481)	0.592 (0.494)
FDA regulation (0–1) ($n=83, 110$)	0.473* (0.502)	0.337* (0.476)
EPA regulation	0.524 (0.500)	0.469 (0.502)
OSHA regulation (0–1)	0.213 (0.411)	0.255 (0.438)

[a]Means; standard errors of mean are given in parentheses.
*   Two-tailed test, significant at the 10% level.
**   Two-tailed test, significant at the 5% level.
*** Two-tailed test, significant at the 1% level.
Source: Viscusi and Hakes (1997).

in large part to the synthetic character of the risk.[4] Environmental and occupational regulations are more in line with the expected pattern, with chemicals found to be carcinogenic more likely to be regulated.

Panel (*b*) gives a profile of chemicals based on whether the chemical is synthetic. The synthetic chemicals did not differ in a statistically significant manner in terms of their carcinogenicity measured in terms of the 0–1 variable for whether they are found to be carcinogenic or in terms of the rats' TD_{50} value, which is the amount of the chemical needed before 50 percent of the rats in the sample develop tumors (i.e. the toxic dose of the 50th percentile). However, synthetic chemicals are more likely to be regulated, where this difference arises almost exclusively from the greater propensity of food and drug regulations to pertain to them.

The general character of the FDA's response to chemicals is that it is not the risk posed by the chemical that seems to be the driving concern, but rather the chemical's synthetic or natural character. These biases mirror the irrational responses of society at large to novel risks. Moreover, there is no evidence of a significant relationship between actions by regulatory agencies and the size of the risk, which should be a central matter of concern.

CONSERVATISM AND RISK ASSESSMENT

When confronting government risk statistics, there is a tendency to take this information at face value. Presumably, government officials should be a source of accurate risk information. Unfortunately, the practice of risk assessment in the federal government in the United States is not concerned with providing best estimates of the risk or measures of central tendency. Rather, the policy emphasis is on conservative risk assessments, so that risk management and risk analysis become blurred.[5] In effect, policymakers mix policy advocacy with science and do not report the underlying scientific information to enable decision makers to make different judgments.

[4] See Ames, Magaw, and Gold (1987) for discussion of the pertinent scientific issues.

[5] A series of proposed bills that were considered by the 104th Congress attempted to rectify this situation by requiring the use of mean risk values. One prominent example is HR9, which was passed by the US House of Representatives, but not by the US Senate.

Consider the following situation. Suppose there is policy option 1, which saves 500 lives with certainty. The alternative is to pursue policy option 2, which offers a 50–50 chance of saving either 1 life or 501 lives. The policy choice available permits us to pursue only one of these two options.

Policy option 1 saves the greatest expected number of lives and would be the preference of efficiency-oriented economists. However, policy option 2 offers the greatest potential gains and will be chosen if we focus only on the worst-case scenario, which is the current risk analysis approach. Government risk assessment practices that recognize only the maximum possible risk in effect would give policy preference to policy option 2.

Although this might be viewed as the conservative scenario in terms of offering the greatest potential lifesaving gains, even from the standpoint of adopting a 'conservative' policy, this focus appears to be misplaced. If in fact we save only one life with policy option 2, then in effect we have sacrificed 499 additional lives that could have been saved with policy option 1. Thus, the opportunity costs in terms of minimizing the forgone opportunity to save lives will be to pursue policy option 1, rather than the supposedly conservative policy option 2. This perspective on conservatism consequently poses the question in terms of whether being 'conservative' is to maximize the minimum number of lives saved or to minimize the maximum possible number of lives lost. To avoid such anomalies, the general principle that has been the focus of recent proposed legislation in the United States is that the expected number of lives saved should be our policy guide.[6]

How these various conservatism biases get implemented is exemplified in Figure 6.1. The conservatism biases are pervasive throughout the entire analysis. This diagram sketches the manner in which US Environmental Protection Agency (EPA) officials calculate the risks from exposure to contaminated groundwater resulting from hazardous wastes. This example is instructive in that it indicates that the risk assessment biases do not simply involve a single conservatism adjustment factor, which might be easily corrected, but rather permeate the entire analysis.

---

[6] Bills such as HR1022 and HR9 before the 104th Congress adopted this approach, as did many proposed Senate bills such as that proposed by Senator Robert Dole. In 1997 one proposed bill along these lines remained active.

Lifetime excess cancer risk =
Human intake factor × [Concentration] × Toxicity

$$\frac{IR \times EF \times ED}{BW \times AT}$$

IR = Ingestion rate (liters/day)
EF = Exposure frequency (days/yr)
ED = Exposure duration (yrs/'life')
BW = Body weight (kg)
AT = Average time (days in a 'life' (definition))
Chemical concentration (mg/kg)
Toxicity $(\text{mg/kg/day})^{-1}$

FIG. 6.1 Carcinogenic Risk Equation for Groundwater Ingestion

The lifetime excess cancer risk is a product of the human intake factor for the chemical, the concentration of the chemical, and its toxicity. How much of the chemical intake occurs depends on the ingestion rate, the exposure frequency, the exposure duration, the body weight, and the average time of exposure. Thus, there are five components of the risk calculation that enter in the numerator and two in the denominator. In the case of every component in the numerator, EPA uses an upper bound value, which is typically a value such as the 95th percentile amount.

Using 95th percentile values for several component parameters leads to a much greater degree of conservatism in the calculated risk level. The net effect is to compound the conservatism biases, producing a much greater overall degree of conservatism. The biases in EPA hazardous waste calculations, excluding the overestimate of the toxicity of the chemical (i.e. the dose–response relationship), overstate the hazard on average by a factor of 30. Moreover, the estimated risk itself is well beyond the 99th percentile of the risk distribution. Put somewhat differently, there is much less than a 1 percent chance that the risk will be as great as government officials estimate. The result is that these biased risk assessments will distort policymaking, diverting our attention from hazards that are substantial and well known to hazards that are imprecisely understood and which may pose no real threat.

This result is not specific to the hazardous waste cleanup effort known in the United States as the Superfund program. Suppose that one focuses on a series of such parameters, each of which is at the 95th percentile. Assume for simplicity that the parameters are independent and lognormally distributed, which is a commonly estimated norm for such environmental parameters. Compounding conservatism from three parameters will put the assessed risk at the 99.78th percentile of the overall risk distribution. If there are four such parameters, using the 95th percentile for each will put the resulting risk estimate at the 99.95th percentile. Compounding conservatism for component parameters based on the implicit assumption that the worst will always prevail leads to overall risk estimates that are extremely implausible and much more unlikely than the component percentiles. The chance of four 'tails' in a row in successive coin flips is much lower than the chance of getting 'tails' a single time—a quite basic result whose practical implications are not reflected in EPA policy.

The defense of conservatism is that society suffers very substantial losses when outcomes turn out badly.[7] However, this justification hinges on a very special loss function. Table 6.2 presents pertinent information for an illustrative example involving three possible risk levels and their associated probabilities. In the case of the high risk, there is a 0.001 chance that the risk probability will be as great at 0.01 with a social loss of V for each adverse outcome. The value of V could be the value of a life lost or the value of each life times the

TABLE 6.2. Statistics for Conservatism Bias Example

Probability of risk level	Risk level	Expected loss
0.599	0	0
0.400	0.0001	$0.00004V$
0.001	0.01	$0.00001V$
Total		$0.00005V$

[7] See Krier (1990) for articulation of this view.

exposed population. The expected loss for this high risk situation is consequently $0.00001V$ after taking into account the probability that this situation could prevail. One can calculate expected losses similarly for the two lower risk possibilities. Over the entire three states, the total expected loss if $0.00005V$. This value will be reflected in an expected value analysis without considering 'conservatism.'

Justifying a conservatism bias in which one treats 0.01 as the risk level requires more than a belief that society is very concerned with adverse outcomes. That type of influence can be reflected in higher values of V without adopting any conservatism bias that alters the weight on large risk levels. One might, for example, value lives at \$7 million rather than \$3 million if one wanted to place a substantial weight on the benefits of lifesaving activities. The conservatism bias in effect makes the value of V greater only when the risk probability is high. Contrary to standard assumptions underlying expected utility theory, values attached to states and assessed values of probabilities are not independent if one adopts a conservatism bias.

The difficulty in avoiding such biases may stem from a form of 'hindsight bias.' If the risk turns out to be large, surely officials should have recognized it, increasing the political sanctions. These pressures should be resisted if the lives saved when risks are small have the same value as an equal number of lives saved when the risks are large. This type of bias is in fact sometimes reflected in personal risk policies as well, as was discussed in Chapter 4. For example, there may be greater concern (measured by cost per life saved) in avoiding a large number of deaths than avoiding a smaller number of fatalities in a more isolated incident. Publicity per life lost from major catastrophes often dwarfs the attention given to smaller scale accidents.

Conservatism biases enter in other ways as well. The estimated biases above take at face value the government's assumption regarding the likelihood of individual exposure to the risk. In practice, there may be much less chance of exposure than government officials assume. In its risk analyses, EPA officials designate two risk categories: current risks, which are actual or potential risks associated with current land use, and potential risks, which it calls future risks. These future risks are actually a misnomer, in that they are hypothetical future risks that involve a change from the current land use. Vacant land might, for example, be used for a daycare facility in future years. These hypothetical future risks dominate the risks driving policy, as over 91 percent of the total cancer pathway risks involve such future risks. Moreover, the great majority of these future risks involve an assumption by the government agency that there will be on-site exposures of residents to the hazardous wastes. In effect, government officials are assuming that in the future people will voluntarily choose to move onto hazardous waste sites where people do not now live, even though these sites have been designated as sufficiently risky to be on the US Environmental Protection Agency's National Priorities List for cleanup. Such an assumption is contrary to actual behavior, as governmental designation of a hazardous waste site generally leads to population exits and decreased land values.

However, these statistics are consistent with the types of patterns noted by US Supreme Court Justice Stephen Breyer (1993) in his book *Breaking the Vicious Circle*:

Let me provide some examples. The first comes from a case in my own court, *United States v. Ottati & Goss*, arising out of a ten-year effort to force cleanup of a toxic waste dump in southern New Hampshire. The site was mostly cleaned up. All but one of the private parties had settled. The remaining private party litigated the cost of cleaning up the last little bit, a cost of about $9.3 million to remove a small amount of highly diluted PCBs and 'volatile organic compounds' (benzene and gasoline components) by incinerating the dirt. How much extra safety did this $9.3 million buy? The forty-thousand-page record of this ten-year effort indicated (and all the parties seemed to agree) that, without the extra expenditure, the waste dump was clean enough for children playing on the site to eat small amounts of dirt daily for 70 days each year without significant harm. Burning the soil would have made it clean enough for the children to eat small amounts daily for 245 days per year without significant harm. But there were no dirt-eating children playing in the area, for it was a swamp. Nor were dirt-eating children likely to appear there, for future building seemed unlikely. The parties also agreed that at least half of the volatile organic chemicals would likely evaporate by the year 2000. To spend $9.3 million to protect non-existent dirt-eating children is what I mean by the problem of 'the last 10 percent.'[8]

Such risk assessment biases are not restricted to hazardous waste programs. Air pollution regulatory efforts often assume that all plants operate at full capacity. Government policies generally assume that there will be no adaptive responses, such as changes in crop selection or residential land use in response to global climate

---

[8] Breyer (1993), pp. 11–12.

change. These risk assessments also tend to rely on the most sensitive animal species rather than trying to develop the estimates most representative of potential risks to humans. Perhaps most arbitrary is that, even after all these various conservatism biases, risk analysts often multiply the resulting risk estimate by an arbitrary factor, such as an order of magnitude, for the sake of 'conservatism.' Analyses of the risks posed by US drinking water include a whole series of such blowup factors of 10 to account for the extrapolation of animal studies to humans and a wide variety of other uncertainties. Such practices lead to a policy result in which we are in effect lying to ourselves about the risks that are truly present. Honest risk assessment, including information about the distribution of potential risk, is a more reliable guide to policy. Current practices confuse risk assessment with risk management. Stealthy policymakers in effect pre-empt what should be a public social choice by clandestine decisions at the staff analyst level.

THE IRRATIONALITY OF HAZARDOUS WASTE CLEANUP[9]

The full import of hazardous waste cleanup decisions can best be understood by contrasting these choices with an efficient social welfare maximization reference point. The policy decision should maximize social welfare W through selection of the target risk T after cleanup. The baseline risk is B, the exposed population is E, and the value per cancer case avoided is V. The variables affecting the cost C of cleanup include B, T, and the site characteristics S. The policy task is then to

$$\underset{T}{\text{Max}}\ W = (B - T) \times E \times V - C(B,T,S), \qquad (6.1)$$

yielding

$$-dC/dT = E \times V. \qquad (6.2)$$

The savings in marginal costs from a more lenient target equals the marginal benefits lost per unit of the target risk variable—the exposed population weighted by the value per cancer case.

---

[9] The discussion in this section draws on Viscusi and Hamilton (1996).

Because of perceptional biases, policymakers may not perceive either risk levels or exposed populations accurately. The perceived baseline risk B^* may be a function of the actual baseline risk B, the likelihood L of the risk scenario, and various patterns P of perceptional biases. The perceived target risk T^* is also dependent on these variables as well as possibly the baseline risk B. Finally, the effective exposed population E^* may depend on both the actual exposed population E and the nature of the community N. Differences in political clout may give different populations a weight that is disproportionate to their numbers.

The modified optimization problem becomes

$$\underset{T}{\text{Max}}\ \ W^* = \{B^*(B,L,P) - T^*(B,L,P,T)\} \times E^*(E,N) \times V - C(B,S,T), \tag{6.3}$$

which leads to the first-order condition

$$-dC/dT = (\partial T^*/\partial T) \times E^* \times V. \tag{6.4}$$

The perceptional biases that account for the differences between equations (6.2) and (6.4) are those that pertain to the perceived changes in the target risk level—$\partial T^*/\partial T$—and the effective exposed population E^*. Higher values of these variables relative to their accurate perception counterparts (i.e. 1 and E) will lead to a justification of higher marginal cleanup costs and consequently to a more stringent risk target.

As in the case of private risk beliefs, target risk perceptions may overstate the extent of the change in risk when the target risk is zero because of the role of a certainty premium. Similarly, policymakers understate partial reductions in risk. This type of bias is reflected in the strong policy orientation toward complete cleanup irrespective of very large costs. Indeed, there is no incentive to pursue less than complete cleanup if the risk is at least 10^{-4} initially. This policy trigger for definite cleanup action does not serve as a stopping point for cleanup, nor does the 10^{-4} to 10^{-6} discretionary risk range for cleanup. Instead, cleanups often decrease the risk to 10^{-7} or lower in pursuit of the zero risk ideal.

Perceptions of perceived and target risks also embody a variety of conservatism adjustment factors discussed above. The treatment of current populations and hypothetical future risks is a similar type of ambiguity bias. The stringency of the target risk levels selected are not significantly different for current as opposed to future risks. The same general patterns of ambiguity aversion encountered in individual choices are mirrored in government policy.

Individual risk perceptions are also subject to a class of biases known as the 'availability effect.' People tend to overestimate risks that have been the subject of recent experience. In much the same way, after controlling for scientific assessments of the riskiness of chemicals, EPA sets more stringent chemical cleanup targets in instances in which there has been substantial publicity for the site or where the chemicals being regulated have received substantial media coverage (as measured using Lexis news files).

The role of the exposed populations is likewise subject to a variety of biases. Whereas ideally the total exposed population at different risk levels should be components of the policy assessment calculus, governmental risk assessments do not formally recognize the size of the exposed population. The failure to distinguish between current and hypothetical future risk exposures is reflective of a broader emphasis on risk probabilities alone, with no consideration of how many people are exposed. Such concerns do not even enter informally, as there is no statistically significant influence of the size of the exposed population on the cleanup target selected.

This type of bias parallels a form of irrationality found in contingent valuation studies of natural resources. When respondents are asked how much they value saving 100 birds or 10,000 birds, for example, their survey responses are not sensitive to the number of birds. This bias is often discussed under the designation of 'scope effects' or 'embedding effects.' Respondents may be contributing to worthy environmental causes more generally and may not be responding to the specific commodity in question. Similarly, EPA does not take into account the extent of the population at risk in its cleanup decisions.

This type of 'scope effect' bias does not imply, however, that the agency ignores the affected population. Political factors such as local voting rates and the environmental voting ratings of the area's representatives are influential. What is perhaps most disturbing from an economic efficiency standpoint is that political factors have the greatest influence when the risks posed by a site are small and there are no or few exposed people. The influence of political factors consequently is to push policies further from an efficiency ideal and to augment the failures arising from the government's mirroring of patterns of individual irrationality. The extent of the resulting inefficiency is reflected in an average cost per case of cancer prevented of $11.7 billion.[10]

The net effect of these various forms of irrationality is twofold. First, the irrational responses of citizens put pressure on political actors to take actions that reflect the concerns captured by these irrational responses. To the extent that politicians are vote maximizers or are concerned with political support more generally, they will tend to respond to public pressures even though these may not be grounded on a rational perception of risk. The second implication of such phenomena is that policymakers themselves as individuals may exhibit the same kinds of irrationalities, thus tending to reinforce the irrationalities of the public at large. In each case the risk policy outcome will be pushed further from the policies that would be pursued if the objective were to target societal resources in the most cost-effective manner for promoting individual health.

REGULATORY TRADEOFFS

Cost is also a matter of concern. As a society we do not have sufficient resources to eliminate all risks of death. If we were to spend the entire US gross domestic product to eliminate accidental deaths, the total amount that could be spent per accidental death avoided would be only $55 million. That would leave nothing left over for food, housing, or prevention of illnesses.

The need to exercise restraint is reflected in our own decisions. The US Department of Transportation estimates that there are an additional 1,300 deaths per year resulting from the switch to smaller, more fuel efficient cars. By driving cars with less bulk, we necessarily sacrifice some protective capabilities. Doing so is not necessarily irrational, nor is being unwilling to spend substantially more for an automobile that would offer only modestly greater protective capability.

Notwithstanding these limits, US government regulatory policies have been based on legislation that for the most part directs agencies to eliminate risks irrespective of cost. Affordability often enters, but usually in terms of financial feasibility rather than benefit–cost

---

[10] This estimate is for a sample of 150 sites. Evidence on the distribution of the costs per case of cancer appear below. Those figures understate the efficiency loss, as they do not adjust for biases in EPA risk assessments or discount the deferred cases of cancer prevented.

TABLE 6.3. The Cost of Various Risk-Reducing Regulations per Life Saved

Regulation	Year and status	Agency[b]	Cost per life saved millions of 1984 $)
Pass benefit–cost test:			
Unvented space heaters	1980 F[a]	CPSC	0.10
Cabin fire protection	1985 F	FAA	0.20
Passive restraints/belts	1984 F	NHTSA	0.30
Underground construction	1989 F	OSHA	0.30
Alcohol and drug control	1985 F	FRA	0.50
Servicing wheel rims	1984 F	OSHA	0.50
Seat cushion flammability	1984 F	FAA	0.60
Floor emergency lighting	1984 F	FAA	0.70
Crane suspended personnel platform	1988 F	OSHA	1.20
Concrete and masonry construction	1988 F	OSHA	1.40
Hazard communication	1983 F	OSHA	1.80
Benzene/fugitive emissions	1984 F	EPA	2.80
Fail benefit-cost test:			
Grain dust	1987 F	OSHA	5.30
Radionuclides/uranium mines	1984 F	EPA	6.90
Benzene	1987 F	OSHA	17.10
Arsenic/glass plant	1986 F	EPA	19.20
Ethylene oxide	1984 F	OSHA	25.60
Arsenic/copper smelter	1986 F	EPA	26.50
Uranium mill tailings, inactive	1983 F	EPA	27.60
Uranium mill tailings, active	1983 F	EPA	53.00
Asbestos	1986 F	OSHA	89.30
Asbestos	1989 F	EPA	104.20
Arsenic/glass manufacturing	1986 R	EPA	142.00
Benzene/storage	1984 R	EPA	202.00
Radionuclides/DOE facilities	1984 R	EPA	210.00
Radionuclides/elementary phosphorus	1984 R	EPA	270.00
Benzene/ethylbenzenol styrene	1984 R	EPA	483.00
Arsenic/low-arsenic copper	1986 R	EPA	764.00
Benzene/maleic anhydride	1984 R	EPA	820.00
Land disposal	1988 F	EPA	3,500.00
EDB	1989 R	OSHA	15,600.00
Formaldehyde	1987 F	OSHA	72,000.00

[a] F or R=final or rejected rule.
[b] CPSC, Consumer Product Safety Commission; OSHA, Occupational Safety and Health Administration; FAA, Federal Aviation Administration; NHTSA, National Highway Traffic Safety Administration; FRA, Federal Railroad Administration.

Source: Viscusi (1992a), p. 264.

balancing. The result, as is shown in Table 6.3, is that the cost per life saved (shown in the final column) is often exorbitant. For concreteness, let us use a $5 million estimate of the implicit value of life as the benefit–cost threshold. Some regulations, particularly those pertaining to transportation, would pass a benefit–cost test. Other regulations, such as those pertaining to asbestos and many other environmental hazards, would fail a benefit–cost test. Indeed, US executive branch oversight of regulatory policies has failed to reject any regulation with a cost per life saved of under $142 million. Such profligate expenditures not only waste societal resources but also are potentially counterproductive, in that they divert funds that could have greater mortality-reducing effects even if spent on a random mix of consumer items.

One reason why these regulatory expenditures are so wasteful is that virtually all the risk gains produced by the regulation could be produced with the initial set of productive expenditures. Policymakers then push the stringency of desirable regulations too far as there is no concern for benefit–cost balancing.

There has been much discussion in the risk analysis literature of the 90–10 principle.[11] Government agencies may incur 90 percent of the costs to address the last 10 percent of the risk. The initial regulatory expenditures are very effective, but their efficacy drops off very quickly. This hypothesized principle is intended to be not a precise rule of thumb but rather an indication that we can probably achieve most of the risk benefits through fairly modest initial expenditures and avoid the relatively unproductive expenditures while sacrificing little in terms of risk benefits.

To provide an empirical perspective on this hypothesized relationship, James T. Hamilton and I explored this relationship for the US hazardous waste cleanup program, known as Superfund. The dropoff in policy efficacy is even starker than risk analysts have long hypothesized. Table 6.4 summarizes the cost effectiveness of different Superfund expenditures. The first column ranks the expenditures by their relative effectiveness. Thus, the first row consists of those cleanup expenditures that rank in the top 5 percent in terms of their efficacy; the second row consists of those that are in the next 5 percentile grouping; and so on. The striking result of this calculation is

---

[11] See e.g. Breyer's (1993) statement quoted earlier in this chapter. Trade association representatives for polluting firms have been perhaps the most vocal popularizers of this phenomenon.

TABLE 6.4.   Summary of Superfund Cost-Effectiveness

% of remediation program expenditures, ranked by cancer cost effectiveness (*n* = 99)	% of total expected cancers averted[a]	Maginal cost per cancer case averted ($m)[b]
0–5	99.46	137
5–10	99.61	231
10–15	99.74	306
15–20	99.81	731
20–25	99.86	1,044
25–30	99.89	1,189
30–35	99.92	1,673
35–40	99.94	1,902
40–45	99.95	3,306
45–50	99.96	6,072
50–55	99.96	8,248
55–60	99.97	15,105
60–65	99.97	15,261
65–70	99.97	17,714
70–75	99.97	26,635
75–80	99.97	63,677
80–85	99.98	84,884
85–90	99.98	114,913
90–95	99.98	227,220
95–100	99.98	NA: cancers = 0

[a] Cancer cases avoided do not total 100 since in some instances EPA chooses not to adopt a full cleanup policy.
[b] The aggregate cost per cancer case averted for the 15 sites that fall in this category is $389,000.

Source: This table is based on joint research by W. Kip Viscusi and James T. Hamilton. Cost estimates are based on EPA risk assumptions, not adjusted for conservatism bias. Such adjustments would increase the cost per case of cancer estimates by roughly a factor of 30. Cancer cases have been discounted at a 3% rate using an 8-year lag.

that the first 5 percent of expenditures eliminate 99.46 percent of the total expected cases of cancers averted by hazardous waste cleanup efforts. The remaining 95 percent of all cleanup costs achieve virtually nothing in terms of health risk reduction.

Although the *average* cost per case of cancer prevented for the initial 5 percentile grouping is relatively good—$389,000—by the time one hits the 5th percentile the *marginal* cost per case of cancer prevented has risen to $137 million. Moreover, by the time we hit the 25th percentile the marginal cost per case of cancer has escalated above $1 billion. In effect, virtually all the agency's cleanup resources are being squandered on cleanups that have a negligible relationship to individual health.

In contrast, if these expenditures were allocated to more mundane kinds of risk regulation policies, such as improved guardrails on highways, we could save substantially more lives at much less cost. The US Department of Transportation, for example, refuses to pursue any regulation with a cost per life saved in excess of $3 million. The median cost per life saved for Superfund cleanup efforts is over $6 billion per case of cancer prevented, and the mean value is $11.7 billion. We could achieve more than a several thousand-fold increase in the number of lives saved per dollar spent by shifting our focus from wasteful policies such as Superfund to more fundamental health and safety efforts.

REGULATORY PERFORMANCE

What has been the payoff from this flurry of regulatory activity that has taken over the US regulatory agenda over the past quarter century?[12] Figure 6.2 indicates the trend in many major accident patterns, which I have analyzed in detail elsewhere.[13] The advent of most regulatory efforts, such as those pertaining to work accidents, began in the early 1970s. Yet, there is little apparent shift in the trends that economists have been able to link to regulatory policies. Much of the source of decreased risk has stemmed from the increased societal wealth, which in turn has increased our demand for safety.

What matters from an evaluative standpoint is the shift in the trend in risk from its predicted level taking other factors into account. The considerable economics literature on this issue indicates that the effects of risk regulation policies have tended to be small, though they now appear to be nonzero. Thus, there does

---

[12] Morrall (1981) provides the first comprehensive review.

[13] Viscusi (1992*a*) and related articles cited therein address these issues. Kniesner and Leeth (1995) provide a sophisticated analysis of job safety policies, and Jones-Lee (1989) provides a comprehensive assessment of transport safety regulation.

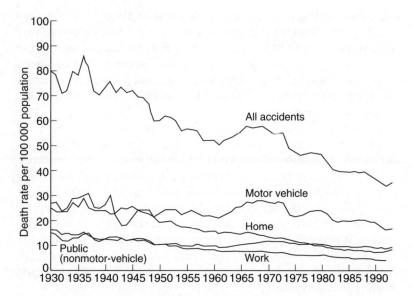

Fɪɢ. 6.2 Trends in Accidental Death Rates in the United States, 1930–1993
Source: Based on data from National Safety Council (1994), pp. 24, 26–7.

appear to be some modest beneficial safety effect. The question that now must be resolved by policymakers is how to better design these efforts to strike a more reasonable balance between cost and risk and to focus these expenditures in a way that will produce the greatest risk reduction benefits for the money expended.

THE LEGISLATIVE AGENDA

The year 1996 was a period of major debate in the United States involving a legislative overhaul that would restructure the focus of regulatory agencies.[14] The concerns that were the object of this political debate are of particular interest to economists since they focused

[14] A regulatory reform bill was passed by the US House of Representatives but not by the Senate. In 1997 one US Senate proposal remained active, but the prominence of the regulatory reform debate had decreased.

almost exclusively on economic methodology used to evaluate regulatory programs. Thus, there was an unusual interest in economic substance that went beyond the typical level of political discourse.

As one might expect, a major issue is whether the benefits of regulatory policies must exceed their costs. That policies should, on balance, be in society's best interest would seem to be a broadly innocuous criterion. However, implementing such a criterion through legislation raises new concerns. For example, must all benefits and costs be monetized? If they are not, how will such a requirement be enforced either through action by other branches of the government itself or through judicial actions? Current policies do not generally recognize such balancing. The weaker variants of proposed legislation that would at least permit the agencies to compare benefits and costs and to require that benefits and costs bear a reasonable relationship would be a stark shift from policies now in place.

The second major component of the policy reforms is the provision for honest risk assessment. Rather than providing only upwardly biased conservative risk assessments, policymakers would now be required to present mean risk values as well. Moreover, if they are going to provide estimates of the upper bound of the risk, they must also provide estimates of the lower bound of the risk so that it will be possible to obtain a greater sense of the overall distribution.

A third interesting component of the reform proposals is the inclusion of risk–risk analysis. Many legislators have recognized the importance of substitution risks whereby, for example, if we require that infants traveling on planes be ticketed in a separate seat, then many people will choose to drive, thus posing an even greater risk. Moreover, behavioral responses to regulation such as seatbelts, safety caps, and cigarette lighters would also have to be taken into account when computing the net risk effects. The potential for wasteful regulatory expenditures to, in effect, make us worse off by squandering resources that would have had greater mortality-reducing effects if not spend on regulatory policies also would be a component of the risk–risk approach.

Some of the controversies that derailed the passage of such legislation did not pertain to economics but rather to institutional practices that would have slowed down the pace of regulation. These proposals included institutional reforms that provided for peer review panels to address major regulatory proposals, retrospective studies of the performance of regulations, and explicit provisions for judicial challenges to regulatory proposals.

Although efforts to reform regulatory policy have not yet met with success, there is a broader recognition of the importance of ensuring that these major regulatory expenditures do in fact generate the kinds of risk reduction benefit that we should demand from these considerable costs. The current relatively indiscriminate approach to regulatory policy has passed up many more profitable opportunities for saving lives through the lack of focus on the efficacy of different risk reduction opportunities.

The current policy failures are neither accidental nor malicious. However, in their singleminded zeal to reduce risk, policymakers have fallen prey to the same types of failure of rationality that are embodied in personal risk-taking decisions. The extent to which these biases arise because the irrationality of citizens creates regulatory pressures or policymakers as individuals are irrational is not clear. From a political standpoint, responding to citizen fears may be a 'rational' political act that maximizes popular support, but it may not foster more rational societal risk decisions.

Unfortunately, the outcome is that risk policies now institutionalize private decision failures. Regulatory practices unduly penalize new risks, fail to recognize the risk from natural as opposed to synthetic chemicals, embody a wide variety of conservatism biases, ignore the extent of the population protected (scope effects), and are unduly influenced by the media (availability effect) and political pressures.

The hazardous waste cleanup experience reflects the extent of current policy failures. Hazardous wastes rank number one on the public's list of environmental fears and serve as the popular symbol of worthwhile environmental policies.[15] The risks from hazardous wastes have become so distorted in the public's view and in regulatory actions that policies now squander our risk reduction resources. For every case of cancer prevented by hazardous waste cleanup,

[15] In his first presidential candidate debate with Senator Robert Dole on October 6, 1996, President Clinton cited hazardous waste cleanup among his administration's important environmental efforts. Vice President Gore likewise raised Superfund support as an issue in the vice-presidential debate on October 9, 1996. When the 104th Congress failed to quickly renew EPA's budget on schedule, the cessation of hazardous waste cleanup was touted as a major adverse consequence of the budgetary impasse.

comparable expenditures on traffic safety could save thousands of lives, such as that of Arne Ryde.[16]

It is somewhat ironic that policymakers who squander resources most irresponsibly often tout their refusal to recognize tradeoffs and other economic concerns as reflecting a commitment to the environment and public health that places them on a higher moral plane. As the risk–risk analysis discussion demonstrated, wasteful efforts harm public health on balance. The case for marshalling our risk reduction resources to reflect economists' prescriptions for effective resource allocation should not be controversial.

---

[16] Noll and Krier (1990) also examine the political and psychological contributors to irrational risk policies.

7
Liability and Social Insurance

Increasingly, the economic incentives that firms face with respect to risk include not only market forces and the role of government regulation, but also the costs of liability suits. Some firms have reorganized under US bankruptcy laws in response to liability suits pertaining to asbestos and medical devices. Even the most venerable insurance institution, Lloyd's of London, has been restructured to deal with the wave of liability costs. There have also been more subtle changes, such as the removal of diving boards from motels, increased corporate concern with hazard warnings, and greater emphasis on product safety generally. Costs associated with workers' compensation have also escalated tremendously in the United States to a level of $30 billion in premiums per year so that these costs now outweigh more traditional social insurance costs, such as unemployment compensation expenses. The implication of these changes is that, whereas safety concerns were formerly an incidental matter for corporate public affairs offices, they are now at the forefront of corporate policy and often are central to the very survival of the corporation.

The manner in which these influences get transmitted is exemplified by the experience in the Agent Orange litigation. Agent Orange was the herbicide used by the United States to defoliate the jungles in Vietnam. In addition to this beneficial military function, however, it may have adversely affected the soldiers themselves, many of whom were exposed to substantial quantities of this herbicide as part of military operations or through the administration of the herbicide. The soldiers exposed to Agent Orange and their families sued the US government and the Agent Orange producers after the Vietnam War in an attempt to recover for cancer and other medical problems that they claimed were linked to their exposure.

Table 7.1 tracks the effect of various product liability events on both Dow Chemical Company, the major Agent Orange producer, and the group of six chemical companies that produced the chemical.

TABLE 7.1.   The Effect of Agent Orange Suits on the Value of Dow
Chemical and Total Change for the Six Affected Firms

	Change in Value ($m)	
	Same day	10-day period
Yannacone files action suit, Jan. 8, 1979		
Dow Chemical	−60.74	−50.69
Total change	−55.65	−98.42
Judge Pratt rules federal common law applies, Nov. 20, 1979		
Dow Chemical	43.78	−178.83
Total change	28.42	−267.44
Agent Orange suit for $310 million reported in *Wall Street Journal*, May 30, 1980		
Dow Chemical	38.44	−220.68
Total change	−9.78	−37.63
Agent Orange suit reported in Wall Street Journal, July 10, 1980		
Dow Chemical	−80.98	−97.23
Total change	−151.11	−298.27
Judge Weinstein announces decision, May 7, 1985		
Dow Chemical	83.35	300.69
Total change	145.17	683.18

Source: Viscusi and Hersch (1990).

After the filing of the class action suit in 1979, there was a same-day decrease in the value of the firm of $60 million, which is comparable to the effect over a ten-day event window. The reaction to Judge Pratt's ruling that Federal common law applies was not immediate. However, after it was recognized that this ruling bolstered the plaintiffs' chances of successfully waging their lawsuit, there was a $179 million ten-day period loss experienced by Dow Chemical Company and an even greater loss experienced by the entire group of affected firms.

The next two events listed are reports of the litigation in the *Wall Street Journal*, each of which had substantial negative consequences for Dow Chemical Company. Since the May 30, 1980 story linked the Agent Orange suit primarily to Dow Chemical Company, the adverse effect was concentrated on this firm. All but one of the other firms experienced an increase in value as a result of not being listed as one of the principal defendants in the suit. The final Agent Orange event was the decision by Judge Weinstein. This decision was a compromise which imposed relatively modest liability on the affected firms—a settlement of $180 million or an average of $12,000 for each of the 15,000 plaintiffs. This settlement was a modest value because Judge Weinstein was skeptical of the causality linkage, and the market reflected the fact that the company's losses were below previous expectations.

Agent Orange exemplifies the economic consequences of liability suits, but it is not the only such example.[1]

VALUING SAFETY FOR LIABILITY

To establish the appropriate deterrence value for a company generating fatality risks, one should impose a price based on the value of a statistical life considered in Chapter 4.[2] In situations in which the company otherwise has no financial incentives for safety, these values will send the company the price signal needed for it to recognize the health costs of its actions.

Although these value-of-life estimates are now widely and correctly used to value government risk policies, one should recognize what their economic role is. Value-of-life estimates tell us what the total financial incentives per fatality would be to create incentives for safety. That is a quite different issue from asking what amount would be paid to the survivors of the deceased from the standpoint of insuring their economic loss.

A substantial debate over the use of these value-of-life numbers in the courtroom has continued in the United States. Advocates of rising value-of-life estimates, which have been termed 'hedonic,' or quality-adjusted, damages, view them as simply superior estimates to approaches such as the present value of lost earnings. However, the main distinction is not that they are better: rather, they serve a quite different purpose. They address the optimal deterrence value-of-life question, not the optimal insurance of survivors question. The relative emphasis that should be placed on these two objectives

[1] A wide variety of such instances are reviewed in Viscusi and Hersch (1990) and in Viscusi (1991).
[2] Indeed, the stock market effects of liability suits after airplane crashes lead to a larger implicit value of life equal to as much as $50 m. per fatality; see Broder (1990).

varies with the accident context and the salience of the deterrence concerns.

Implicit value-of-life numbers are not pertinent in assessing the appropriate routine level of compensation for accident victims. Such amounts would provide too much insurance that is not highly valued by the deceased. These value-of-life numbers are nevertheless instructive in ascertaining how much a company should invest in safety.

In the 1970s, the Ford Motor Company marketed a small, inexpensive car known as the Pinto. In its quest for a low price, Ford engineers imposed a variety of cost saving measures. One of these involved the location of the gas tank in the rear of the car. The advantage of this location is that moving the gas tank forward would cost an additional $11 per vehicle. The disadvantage was that the car would be vulnerable to explosion upon impact from the rear.

In an effort to formally assess these and other safety concerns, Ford Motor Company carried out the calculations summarized in Table 7.2.[3] The calculations in the first three columns are those made by Ford Motor Company. Ford estimated that in the absence of altering the position of the gas tanks there would be 180 burn deaths, 180 serious burn injuries, and 2100 burned vehicles. It valued these losses at the usual amounts that it paid in liability suits, such as $200,000 per burn death. This amount reflects the average level of product liability awards during that time period, but it greatly underestimates the value of preventing risks to human life. Compensation in the case of court cases after a fatality is typically based on the present value of lost earnings minus the consumption share of the deceased. This value is at least an order of magnitude below the amount people are willing to pay per unit risk to save their lives. As was indicated in Chapter 4, the implicit value-of-life range from the standpoint of accident prevention is $3 million–$7 million, with a midpoint value of $5 million.

Using this value for human life in the fourth column of panel (*a*), Table 7.2 increases the cost of burn deaths from Ford's estimated value of $36 million to $900 million. After similar adjustment for the value of burn injuries, one calculates that the benefits of moving the

---

[3] These calculations were prepared by Ford, but there is some debate as to whether they pertain to risks from vehicle rollover or rear impact. The context is not as important as the nature of the estimates.

TABLE 7.2.   Benefits and Costs of Redesigning the Ford Pinto

(a) Benefit calculations for increased safety in Pinto gas tank design

Outcome of faculty design ($m)	Ford's unit value ($)	Ford's total value	Unit deterrence value ($)	Total deterrence value
180 burn deaths	200,000	36.0m	5.0m	900.0m
180 serious burn injuries	67,000	12.1m	2.5m	450.0m
2,100 burned vehicles	700	1.5m	700	1.5m
Total		49.6m		1352.0m

(b) Cost calculations for increased safety in Pinto gas tank design

No. of units	Unit cost ($)	Total cost[a] ($m)
11m cars	11	121.0
1.5m light trucks	11	16.5
Total		137.5

[a] Excluded is the minor cost component of the lost consumer's surplus of customers who do not buy Pintos because of the $11 price increase

gas tank would have been $1.4 billion, as compared with Ford's estimate of $50 million.

Panel (*b*) indicates the cost associated with the gas tank relocation, which Ford estimated to be $138 million. Using Ford's calculations, the cost outweighed the benefits by more than 2 to 1. Using more accurate assessments of how people themselves value risk, the benefits exceeded the costs by a factor of almost 10.

Even in liability contexts in which value-of-life figures are not appropriate from the standpoint of compensation, they nevertheless have an important role to play in determining how safe to make products. The appropriate rate of tradeoff should be governed by how the people affected by the product value the risk. That is the valuation that would be expressed through the marketplace if consumers were informed of the extent of the product risks. It is noteworthy that, after the publicity given to the court cases against Ford Motor Company, which led to substantial punitive damages awards against Ford, consumer demand for the Pinto plummeted. Ford then dropped the car as part of its product line.

In thinking about what risk components should enter the assessment of the attractiveness of a product, it is useful to think of three different perspectives one might take. Purchasers' concern with the benefits they derive from the product is reflected in their willingness to pay and their purchase cost. Consumer willingness-to-pay amounts will reflect expected injury costs. Whether the product is in fact desirable for the consumer will also depend on the unexpected injury costs that are not already reflected in consumer calculations.

As part of such suits, there is also frequently discussion of the role of corporate profits, taxes paid by the corporation, benefits to other parties, and costs to other parties. Such concerns may be pertinent if one's perspective is that of a social benefit–cost test. However, such tests should be primarily the providence of regulatory agencies that can make a society-wide decision. From the standpoint of individual liability suits, the attractiveness of the product should be based on whether the product promotes consumer welfare using a full information reference point. Extraneous factors, such as the role of corporate profits, do not serve as a justification for products that on balance decrease consumer welfare.

MASS TOXIC TORTS

A phenomenon that has thus far been concentrated primarily in the United States is the rise of mass toxic torts. Companies now face the prospect of thousands of lawsuits for product defects that affect broad consumer groups. Except for the Thalidomide tragedy in Europe, most mass torts have occurred in the United States.

Formerly, these suits did not arise because liability criteria were restricted to situations in which there were manufacturing defects. Such defects by their very nature tend to occur in isolated instances, such as a car with defectively installed brakes. More recently, liability criteria have been broadened to include design defects and problems arising from inadequate warnings. Since these situations involve correlated risks across mass produced consumer products, the net effect is that there are often large groups of injured populations. This difficulty is particularly great in situations in which there is a gestation before the risk becomes apparent, in which case there may be successive waves of exposed population who ultimately will file liability claims.

Figure 7.1 illustrates the magnitude of several major mass toxic torts in the United States. By far the largest of these waves of litigation pertain to asbestos, as there were 190,000 suits against Manville and 150,000 suits against other asbestos companies. The Dalkon Shield intrauterine device was next in line with 210,000 liability suits. More recent suits involving breast implants and, if litigation is successful, cigarettes would also join the leading mass tort actions. It is noteworthy that manufacturers of both breast implants and cigarettes are considering multi-billion trust funds to settle such claims rather than undergo costly litigation.

The relationship of such suits to the overall US court system appears in Figure 7.2. Although product liability litigation escalated overall through 1990, most of the reason for this upsurge was the dramatic increase in asbestos cases. Indeed, from 1987 through 1991

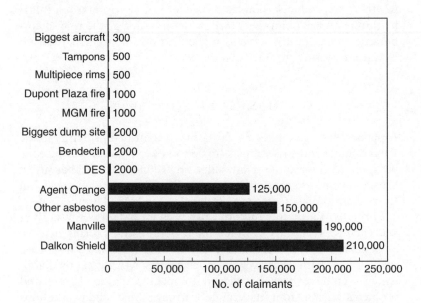

FIG. 7.1 Number of Personal Injury Claimants in Mass Tort Litigation
Source: based on data in Rheingold (1990), p. 15.

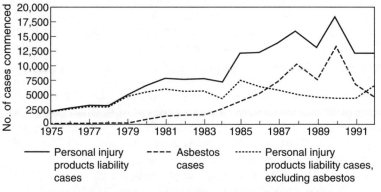

Fig. 7.2 Relative Shares of Asbestos and Nonasbestos Litigation,
1975–1992

there were more asbestos cases filed in US Federal courts than for all
other product risks. Thus, much of the liability crisis can be traced to
the emergence of mass toxic torts.

The difficulties posed by these asbestos suits affected insurance
companies as well. Lloyd's of London was a major insurer of this
asbestos liability. In estimating its prospective risks, in 1982 Lloyd's
estimated that the worst-case scenario would be 81,000 asbestos
claims.[4] By 1990 Lloyd's had increased its estimate of the worst case
scenario to 180,000. Even this estimate reflects an inadequate adjustment to the likely asbestos burden, as the study for the American Bar
Association (see Figure 7.1) estimated the total case load at 340,000
claims. The insolvency problems experienced by many of the Lloyd's
'names' who now face bankruptcy because of asbestos insurance liability has stemmed from the persistent underestimation of the extent
of the asbestos liability burden.

One difficulty that mass toxic torts pose for insurers arises because
in this instance the US court system imposed liability retroactively.
In particular, liability criteria developed after the asbestos exposure
and after the insurance policies were written were then applied to
determine the firm's liability. At the time the risk arose, firms did not
face financial incentives through the liability system to provide
appropriate deterrence. Imposing such liability after the fact serves a

---

[4] These various estimates of the prospective losses are based on the estimates prepared by Sinfield (1994).

compensatory function and will establish a mechanism for future deterrence, but it does not provide incentives for decisions taken earlier. Similarly, since insurance firms cannot charge insurance premiums retroactively, this shift in the liability system created considerable difficulties for insurers as well.

As a practical matter, insurers have responded by changing the way insurance policies for future risks are written. For example, many insurance companies refuse to write environmental risk coverage altogether. Moreover, those that do generally cover only those risks arising within a specified period as opposed to risks attributable to exposures within a particular time period.

Another class of difficulties associated with the asbestos litigation is that the risks are not independent and identically distributed risks, which is the usual characteristic of a nicely diversified risk portfolio. Lloyd's of London had gained a reputation for insuring idiosyncratic risks. While he was a college student at Duke University, basketball player Grant Hill (who later became an NBA rookie of the year and the leading vote getter for the NBA all-star team) purchased insurance for possible career-threatening injury. Famous pianists insure their hands, and Jamie Lee Curtis insured her legs when undertaking a risky commercial. Idiosyncratic risks such as these are not positively correlated, so that insurance of such person-specific hazards is a much less risky enterprise than writing insurance in a situation in which there will be massive numbers of correlated risks.

One potential difficulty in estimating the ultimate asbestos liability burden is that asbestos-related diseases are not signature diseases. With the exception of mesothelioma (cancer of the lining of the lung), diseases caused by asbestos cannot be specifically traced to asbestos exposures. As a result, the courts' compensation of all lung cancer victims who formerly worked with asbestos may ultimately compensate an order of magnitude more plaintiffs than are deserving of compensation because of their asbestos exposures. Predicting the ultimate asbestos burden consequently requires some assessment of how expansive courts will be in awarding damages.

Perhaps the most fundamental problem exhibited by Lloyd's and other insurance companies is that they either do not do systematic actuarial studies (as is often the case with Lloyd's), or they operate as classical statisticians, not as Bayesians. This bias stems in part from insurance regulators' emphasis on historical data. Forecasts based on historical experience will be far from the mark in situations in which there has been a major shift in the risk regime. Situations in which liability rules are undergoing massive changes will not be adequately addressed unless one does more than extrapolate from past experience to construct a sensible predictive model of how current changes will affect future insurance costs. Examination of the asbestos liability trends before 1980 (see Figure 7.2) may give firms a sense of complacency that will not ultimately be warranted once the full implications of the shift in legal rules is transmitted.[5]

The adherence to classical statistical models imposes a kind of rigidity on the forecasting process that in effect is a prescription for bankruptcy. Firms are not able to charge premiums *ex post* to compensate for forecasting errors. The rise of mass toxic torts has greatly increased the stakes involved with such errors.

THE INTERACTION BETWEEN LIABILITY AND ASBESTOS REGULATION

The presence of multiple societal institutions dealing with risk creates the potential for institutional overlaps. Diversification of institutions is often useful in promoting different societal objectives. The court system and social insurance can provide insurance after the fact, whereas government regulation may be better suited for influencing the risk itself. The presence of multiple institutions, however, creates a potential for institutional overlaps in inefficiencies as well. Not all such overlaps may be undesirable, since some redundancy promotes contestability and possibly innovative strategies.

Figure 7.3 illustrates the situation that arose with respect to asbestos. During the period in which asbestos was unregulated and there were massive asbestos exposures, such as the shipyard workers during World War II, individuals faced an inefficiently high risk level. Moreover, since knowledge of the risk was fragmentary, there was not adequate market compensation. These exposures to unregulated risks have given rise to the risk outcomes from inefficiently high risk levels, which have been the object of the liability suits in the courts.

[5] Other insurance company practices may be suspect as well. For example, insurance companies tend to exclude high loss outliers from the analysis as being unrepresentative. The practical result is that, in situations in which losses are highly variable, insurance companies often underestimate the average risk because the high loss cases have been excluded. For documentation see Viscusi (1993).

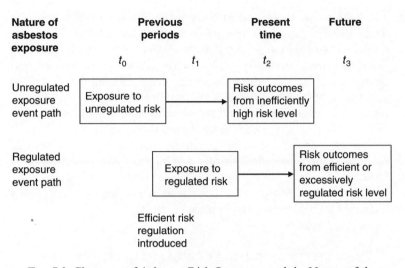

FIG. 7.3 Character of Asbestos Risk Outcomes and the Nature of the
Exposure

Perhaps in part because of the substantial public attention focused on asbestos as a result of these liability suits, government regulators also introduced direct regulation of asbestos beginning in the 1970s. The cost per case of cancer prevented through these regulations has now risen to the $100 million per case level for regulations by both the US Environmental Protection Agency and the US Occupational Safety and Health Administration. Current individuals exposed to asbestos are now being exposed to a risk that is at or below its efficient level in terms of the tradeoff being made between risk and cost. To impose additional liability on asbestos firms in this instance will foster safety incentives even further. This additional incentive will not be efficient given the already stringent level of regulatory policy.

The major difficulty that has arisen with respect to asbestos is that a truly major hazard that was the subject of the societal inattention for many years has now become the focal point of risk control efforts by a variety of societal institutions. Instead of this focused approach, in which there is an inordinate concentration of effort on particularly widely publicized hazards, it would be preferable to have a division of labor in which there is less regulatory attention to risks already addressed adequately through other societal mechanisms. Public pressures for action do not, however, foster this diversified approach but instead establish incentives for institutional overkill.

One mechanism that has not been adequately exploited with respect to asbestos has been the market mechanism. The major asbestos exposures occurred during a period in which the risks of cancer were not widely known. If workers had had information with respect to asbestos risks, would their responses have been sufficient to promote an efficient risk level?

TABLE 7.3. The Effect of Hazard Warnings for Asbestos on Worker Behavior

Variable	Mean value
Initial risk assessment before seeing the warning (0–1 probability scale)	0.09
Risk assessment after receiving the warning (0–1 probability scale)	0.26
Workers refusing to stay on the job at any wage after receiving the warning (fraction)	0.11
Workers intending to quit if given no wage increase after receiving the warning (fraction)	0.65
Workers who would take the job again if given no wage increase after receiving the warning (fraction)	0.11
Additional wage premium for risk required (1995 $)	$4.734
Implicit value of an injury (value per statistical injury) (1995 $)	$27,846

The data in Table 7.3 indicate how workers respond to a well designed asbestos warning. After receiving the warning, their assessed risk in terms of equivalent risks of injury on the job rise from 0.09 to 0.26. Most workers would refuse to stay on the job without a wage increase, and some would refuse to stay on the job at any wage. The average wage premium that workers would require to work on the job is $4,734 (1995 dollars). The implicit value per worker injury equivalent that workers would receive consequently would be $27,846, which is roughly comparable to labor market estimates of the value that workers place on injuries overall. These estimates suggest that workers' valuation of safety in the presence of adequate hazard warnings can provide efficient levels of incentives for accident prevention. Informed market operations not only provide efficient incentives for safety, but also provide compensation for those bearing the risk. Regulations alter safety levels but do not promote compensation unless they also inform workers of risks that they would not otherwise consider.

Non-economists may view the market mechanism as less direct and less satisfactory than direct regulation. However, the fact that the wage incentive is a seemingly less direct mechanism makes it no less potent as a financial incentive. Compensating differentials are the main financial force for safety in the market, with a value for the US economy in excess of $125 billion. Moreover, the advantage of the hazard warnings approach is that in the presence of such warnings conveying risk information, workers will receive additional compensating differentials. Thus, there will be *ex ante* compensation for bearing the risk. In contrast, government regulation that does not also alert workers to the presence of the hazard will alter the risk but will not at the same time compensate workers. Hazard warnings consequently offer the possibility of a superior form of intervention which promotes the dual objectives of compensation and risk incentives rather than providing risk incentives alone.

CIGARETTE LITIGATION

The latest wave of litigation that threatens to have tremendous financial implications is litigation with respect to the hazards of smoking. Thirty percent of US adults continue to smoke, and in many countries the percentage is even higher. Since roughly one-third of these smokers may die because of their smoking activity, the potential for substantial liability stakes is considerable.

The same kind of problems arising in asbestos compensation would arise if the courts compensated smokers. Perhaps one-third of all smokers will die because they smoke, but we do not know who they are. Except for some notable exceptions, such as accidents, most deaths of smokers have at least some causal linkage with smoking. Former smokers may also be able to collect under a broadly defined and ultimately unwieldy compensation system.

A more prominent line of litigation has been the recent wave of suits by a variety of states to recoup those losses associated with the higher cigarette-related medical costs. Smoking has adverse health effects, increasing governmental medical expenditures. These costs have formed the basis for what is now the largest wave of cigarette litigation. In 1997 the parties proposed a \$368.5 billion legislative settlement to resolve the dispute.

Excise taxes on cigarettes can serve two functions: to correct for any errors in misperceptions, and to account for the role of social costs. Suppose $W(Y)$ is the utility of income Y when not smoking, $U(Y-C)$ is the utility of smoking that costs C if smoking does not harm health, and $V(Y-C)$ is the utility of smoking if there is an adverse health effect. Let p be the actual risk of an adverse health effect and let $P(p)$ be the perceived risk. Suppose there is also a social cost S associated with adverse smoking consequences.

The private decision to smoke is governed by whether

$$(1 - P(p))U(Y-C) + P(p)V(Y-C) > W(Y), \tag{7.1}$$

whereas the social desirability of smoking is determined by whether

$$(1-p)U(Y-C) + pV(Y-C) - pS > W(Y). \tag{7.2}$$

Since $P(p)$ may be below p, though generally it is not, and smokers don't recognize the value of S, excise taxes T can better align these values by setting T so that

$$(1 - P(p))U(Y-C-T) + P(p)V(Y-C-T) = (1-p)U(Y-C) \\ + pV(Y-C) - pS. \tag{7.3}$$

Excise taxes can discourage smoking in much the same way as would higher risk perceptions or proper recognition of the externalities. In addition to making private choices potentially efficient socially, they also raise funds that can help defray any social cost S. The empirical issue then is, how should we assess the magnitude of S, and what is its magnitude?

The presence of societal costs is an interesting economic issue because of the presence of competing effects. Although the risks of smoking may generate higher medical costs, the shortened longevity of smokers has cost implications as well.

Figure 7.4 summarizes my estimates of the costs per pack of cigarettes for the US economy. The primary focus is on insurance costs. Cleanup costs for emptying ashtrays and the annoyance of smelling cigarette smoke are among the types of cost not included. The higher medical care costs are \$0.55 per pack, \$0.37 of which is for those

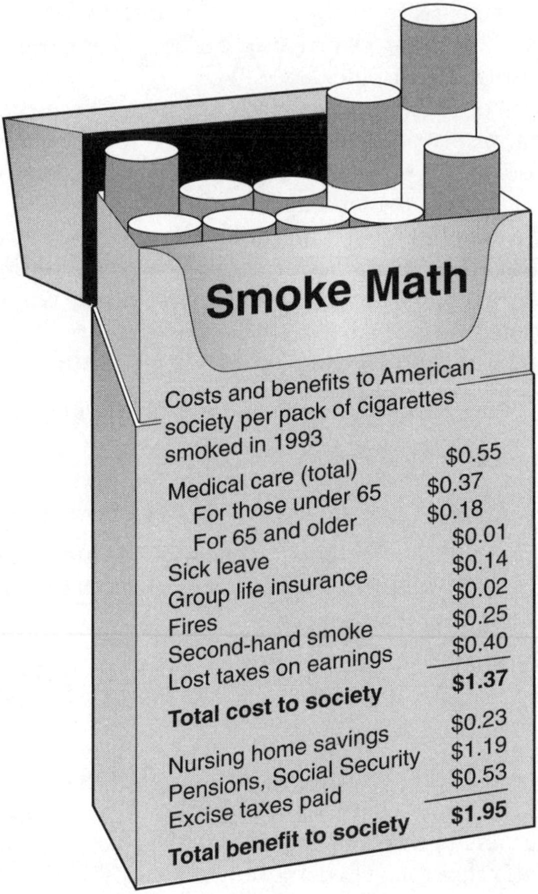

Smoke Math

Costs and benefits to American
society per pack of cigarettes
smoked in 1993

Medical care (total)	$0.55
For those under 65	$0.37
For 65 and older	$0.18
Sick leave	$0.01
Group life insurance	$0.14
Fires	$0.02
Second-hand smoke	$0.25
Lost taxes on earnings	$0.40
Total cost to society	**$1.37**
Nursing home savings	$0.23
Pensions, Social Security	$1.19
Excise taxes paid	$0.53
Total benefit to society	**$1.95**

FIG. 7.4 The Social Costs of Cigarette Smoking, 1993

under age 65, and the remainder is for those 65 and over. The other
major cost components are the $0.40 per pack cost arising from lost
taxes on earnings (including only the contributions to retirement
pensions and medical insurance) because of smokers' early death, the
$0.25 per pack cost arising from environmental tobacco smoke,

which remains much debated,[6] and the $0.14 per pack cost of group life insurance.

Although cigarettes pose a total cost to society of $1.37 per pack, there are offsetting financial ramifications as well. In addition to paying $0.53 per pack in excise taxes, smokers save societal resources through their premature death. In particular, the discounted value of nursing home savings is $0.23 per pack, and the discounted savings of pension and social security costs is $1.19 per pack.

On balance, there is a net financial savings to society from smoking. These estimates do not imply that smoking should be encouraged. Most importantly, these calculations exclude losses to the smokers themselves, which are not the subject of this particular line of litigation. However, they suggest that, if one's only concern is with financial ramifications, then a comprehensive tally indicates that the smokers in effect pay for themselves. The fact that smoking is risky and, in fact, quite deadly has financial consequences, as does the greater frequency of illnesses among smokers.[7]

In addition to helping balance the financial tally between the societal benefits and costs of smoking, excise taxes for cigarettes serve an additional function. In particular, they discourage smoking in much the same way as would higher risk perceptions. Using an estimated price elasticity of demand of −0.4, the average risk equivalent of cigarette taxes in the United States is the same as the lung cancer risk perception of 0.17.[8] For highly price sensitive population groups, such as teenagers—for whom the price elasticity may be as great as −1.4—the lung cancer risk equivalent of cigarette taxes is 0.51. Thus an additional function of the role of cigarette taxes is to discourage smoking in much the same way as would higher risk perceptions.

---

[6] These estimates are based on the midpoint risk estimates by the US Environmental Protection Agency and the US Occupational Safety and Health Administration. It should be emphasized that these are the best governmental estimates presented to date and remain highly uncertain and the subject of substantial scientific disagreement. Cost estimates pertaining to the low and high end of the estimated risk range also appear in Viscusi (1995).

[7] The resolution of these suits remains a matter of controversy, notwithstanding the fact that the financial benefits to society exceed the costs. In particular, the distribution of the cost savings to different segments of society is an issue, since the Federal government benefits primarily from the pension and social security cost savings, whereas the states pay substantial medical care costs without the same extent of an offset. Which cost components will be recognized by the courts and whether the courts will approach these costs on a net basis or by focusing only on selective cost components has yet to be resolved.

[8] These results are based on Table 5.7 of Viscusi (1992*b*).

WORKERS' COMPENSATION

The experience with the workers' compensation program is particularly instructive in that the empirical work on this program enables us to provide a solid empirical basis for many hypothesized economic linkages involved. This social insurance effort illustrates that financial incentives for safety matter to companies and that workers also respond to the compensation package they receive.

Consider the most fundamental issue, whether economic incentives matter. Workers' compensation premiums increase with the riskiness of the firms, where this linkage is particularly strong for large firms. My empirical estimates with Michael Moore indicate that workers' compensation reduces worker fatality rates by almost 30 percent.[9] Put somewhat differently, there would be an additional 1,200 deaths per year on the job were it not for the financial incentives provided by workers' compensation. By, in effect, merit rating firms based on their accident records, workers' compensation provides firms with incentives for safety that in turn result in higher levels of safety for the affected firms. This linkage has provided the empirical basis for a wide variety of other policy proposals, such as those pertaining to medical malpractice reforms.[10]

The workers' compensation experience is also instructive in indicating who pays the cost for liability insurance efforts. In market contexts, compensation for injuries and illnesses will be valued by the prospective recipients and will lead to market effects. In the case of workers' compensation, the provision of compensation for job injuries by firms will make suffering these injuries less harmful to workers, thus decreasing the wage that they will require to work on a risky job.

The empirical evidence for the workers' compensation system indicates that these incentives are quite substantial. Indeed, the wage offset exceeds the total value of workers' compensation premiums.[11] This result is not an anomaly, as it indicates that people who are risk-averse will value insurance at greater than its actuarial value. The same kind of result arises in conventional insurance markets since

---

[9] See Moore and Viscusi (1990*a*).
[10] See Weiler (1991), who cites the workers' compensation experience in making the case for his proposed medical malpractice reforms.
[11] Viscusi and Moore (1987).

insurance must necessarily be actuarially unfair in order to cover administrative costs and normal corporate profits.

The wage offset from workers' compensation is also interesting in that the extent of the wage–workers' compensation tradeoff provides an index of whether the level of benefits is adequate. Let the worker wage rate be denoted by w_1, the workers' compensation benefit level after an injury w_2, and job risk p. Let U^1 be the utility function in the good health state and U^2 the utility function after an injury. The worker's expected utility Z is given by

$$Z = (1-p)U^1(w_1) + pU^2(w_2). \tag{7.4}$$

The theory of compensating differentials is that the job must be sufficiently attractive to equal some constant expected utility level z_0 offered by a safe job. Thus, workers are constant expected utility takers rather than wage takers. On a constant expected utility locus, workers will have a tradeoff between wages and workers' compensation benefits given by

$$\frac{dw_1}{dw_2} = \frac{-\partial Z/\partial w_2}{\partial Z/\partial w_1} = \frac{-pU_x^2}{(1-p)\,U_x^1}. \tag{7.5}$$

However, if workers face actuarially fair insurance rates, they will shift resources across states until they equalize the marginal utility of income across the two health states.[12] The two marginal utility terms in equation (7.5) cancel, leading to the result that workers will choose to select workers' compensation benefits until the rate of tradeoff between workers' compensation and wages equals the relative odds of the two states of the world, or:

$$\frac{-dw_1}{dw_2} = \frac{p}{1-p}. \tag{7.6}$$

By analyzing the extent of the tradeoff, it is consequently possible to determine whether benefits are sufficiently great. This result therefore serves as an empirical test of whether the level of social insurance benefits is efficient. In the case of workers' compensation, the rate of tradeoff exceeds what would be desired on an efficiency basis, indicating that benefit levels are suboptimal. Even after adjusting for insurance loading, the rate of tradeoff is too great, where the counterpart of equation (7.6) in the insurance loading case is:

[12] This variation of the well known insurance result is derived for the job risk case in Viscusi (1979).

$$\frac{-dw_1}{dw_2} = \frac{p(1+a)}{1-p},\qquad(7.7)$$

where a reflects the degree of insurance loading; i.e., the insured worker must sacrifice \$$(1 + a)$ of compensation in the healthy state to provide for \$1 of benefits after an injury.

More specifically, for each extra \$1 in benefits workers sacrifice \$0.12 in wages. This amount exceeds the \$0.05 offset per \$1 tradeoff that is optimal given current insurance loading rates and the \$0.04 offset that would prevail if insurance were actuarially fair.[13]

These wage offset amounts are of substantial policy interest since they indicate that workers in effect pay for workers' compensation through lower wages. This linkage had long been the theoretical justification for many recent developments in tort liability law generally. However, it lacked empirical support until recently.

The existence of a wage offset exceeding the actuarial cost and, consequently, expected benefits is not irrational. All private insurance that is sold has this characteristic. People pay an insurance premium because they are risk-averse. Ideally, one should continue to increase workers' compensation benefits until equation (7.7) is satisfied. Existing tradeoff rates suggest that benefit levels are suboptimal.

Such suboptimal provision of benefits may, however, be warranted in a market context if there are major moral hazard problems with respect to worker injuries. However, since social insurance benefits are not the result of private worker bargains but instead are determined through government policy, it is useful to apply a market-based test to assess whether the insurance levels being provided are optimal.

In part because of the successes of the workers' compensation experience, commentators on liability insurance often recommend that difficult issues such as toxic torts be addressed through an administrative compensation scheme such as workers' compensation. One should, however, be cautious in generalizing from the workers' compensation experience. Much of the reason for the success of workers' compensation has been its focus on safety issues involving acute accidents. Health risks and illnesses pose problems of causality for workers' compensation as well. Solving these problems

---

[13] See Viscusi and Moore (1987) for documentation of this result.

may require more fundamental changes than simply shifting the responsible institutional structure.

CONCLUSION

At least in terms of US risk policy, the focal point for government intervention has shifted over time. In the 1970s, the dominant role was played by the newly emerging regulatory policies. These efforts marked the most direct government intrusion in workplace safety and corporate decisions involving risk. The government programs of much greater duration, such as requirements for health and safety records in the United Kingdom that go back at least to the 1800s, involve less governmental control of workplace operations and characteristics.

Although the cost of regulation continued to remain substantial, in the 1980s the role of the tort liability system escalated dramatically. Product liability premiums in the United States tripled over the 1984–6 period. Whereas firms generally regarded regulations as a costly nuisance, liability costs often had more catastrophic consequences as firms that were the object of a major wave of litigation faced bankruptcy and, in many more limited circumstances, were forced to discontinue major product lines.

The presence of two major institutional structures promoting societal interest in risk creates additional complications as well. Three major institutional structures now provide incentives for risk reductions: the market, government regulation, and tort liability. Ideally, the role of regulation and liability should be to address market failures in a manner that is not duplicative. In practice, however, the same kinds of risk event that often generate substantial liability costs also create considerable pressures for regulatory intervention. The task for the policymakers administering these efforts is to design them in a manner that promotes efficient levels of safety and compensation given the operation of the other institutions involved, rather than to take the institutionally myopic view that no other social structures to promote risk reduction exist.

8

Toward a Rational Basis for Regulation

These lectures in May 1996 took place almost exactly on the twenty-fifth anniversary of the advent of the major wave of health and safety regulation in the United States.[1] After a quarter of a century of experience with these efforts, which by their very nature should be designed to alleviate market failures, it is noteworthy that the major policy question is how these regulatory policies can be reformed to better promote society's interests. The task is to make risk policies a constructive and sensible force for safety rather than to continue the costly and relatively ineffective policies of the past.

As a general rule, the focal point for policy design should be to structure policies to overcome the irrationalities and failures of the market rather than to institutionalize them. Government policies often do not promote balanced decisions but instead function in a reactive manner that often mirrors the kinds of irrationality that have been identified with individual decisions.

The previous chapters have documented a variety of major classes of failure in individual decisions. People frequently make alarmist responses to small risks and exaggerate their importance. However, government policies do much the same thing as they fail to distinguish magnitudes of the risk level and often trigger interventions based on the presence of any evidence of carcinogenicity or similar kind of risk. Policymakers may be reflecting the irrationalities of their consistency, or they may be acting as individuals who themselves display such irrationalities. Responding to irrational public pressures may be 'rational' behavior but bad policy.

Substantial publicity, whether it is generated through actual risk outcomes or liability suits, also tends to create public overestimation of hazards. In market contexts, such overestimation will lead to more

---

[1] For example, the Occupational Safety and Health Administration began operation on April 28, 1971, twenty-five years and less than one month before these lectures.

than sufficient responses to the risk so that the market can be relied upon to promote safety. However, often highly publicized risks do not pose substantial risks to health but instead reflect excessive reactions to minor hazards. The result is that the political pressures for government action are often the greatest when the need for government policies is least. The focus of risk policies should be on those risks that are not handled adequately by the market, not on risks that are so salient that individual decisions will be sound.

The presence of ambiguity aversion to imprecisely understood risks of a loss, which is the loss counterpart of the Ellsberg paradox, is a form of irrationality exhibited in individual behavior. However, government conservative risk assessment practices institutionalize such biases and distort policy decisions. By replacing such conservative risk assessments, which are often boosted by arbitrary conservative adjustment factors with mean risk assessments, policymakers can better promote efforts that save the greatest expected number of lives instead of diverting resources toward small risks that are imprecisely understood.

Another kind of bias that researchers have identified with respect to individual choices is that of 'scope effects.' In valuing environmental goods in contingent valuation surveys, people may not be responsive to the extent of the quantity being valued. The government is also subject to similar anomalies, as it often fails to consider the size of the population exposed to risk and simply focuses on the risk probability.

Similarly, individuals often respond asymmetrically to risk, with increases in accustomed levels of risk and novel risks generating extreme reactions. The government likewise targets novel risks in a variety of ways such as through its inordinate emphasis on avoiding errors of commission with respect to new prescription drugs and the excessive regulation of synthetic chemicals as compared with similarly dangerous natural chemicals.

In addition to avoiding such institutionalization of private irrationalities, government policies can foster the kinds of outcome that would have transpired had markets been efficient. Hazard warning efforts to promote sound assessments of risk can foster more rational individual decisions. Similarly, the government can achieve balance in policies by reflecting the tradeoffs people would have made had markets functioned perfectly.

The role of individual choice is often a missing element in regulatory policy design. Government regulators who frequently proclaim the inadequacies of technologies often rely on technological solutions to safety. By neglecting the influence of people in the accident-generating process, such policies often achieve much less reduction than they could have done had they exploited the role of individual safety behavior in promoting safety.

More than at any time since the inception of the new wave of social regulation, there is now a belief that these efforts should generate risk benefits commensurate with their costs. Economic principles for sound regulation are now at the forefront of the policy debate. Promoting sound risk policies involves more than simply a concern with not wasting money. Poorly designed regulatory policies sacrifice more beneficial opportunities for saving lives. The level of inefficiency of many current regulations is so great that they have less of a beneficial effect on individual health than these expenditures would have had had they simply funded a standard bundle of consumer choices rather than a focused risk regulation effort. Well intentioned but ineffective risk regulations should not be viewed as morally or ethically superior. Wasteful regulatory efforts in effect kill people who would otherwise have benefitted from more health-enhancing private expenditures. Such policies fail any test of viability, even if one's sole concern is with risk reduction.

The rise of multiple societal institutions concerned with risk creates potential opportunities for more effective control of risk, but it creates the potential for new problems as well. Political pressures often generate duplicative incentives for institutional intervention, particularly for regulation and tort liability. Although some institutional competition may be desirable, ideally we should coordinate institutional responses to avoid overlaps and to promote complementary functions. We would not, for example, want several institutions to provide compensation for the same loss in a manner that leads to double dipping.

The shortcomings in societal responses to risk do not imply that regulatory interventions should be abandoned and that companies should be exempt from tort liability. These social institutions for reducing and compensating risk have a legitimate role to play. However, current efforts frequently fall prey to the same kinds of irrationality that plague individual decisions. To fully realize policies' potential, we need to better focus these efforts so that they will promote more balanced and sensible responses to risk.

References

Adams, J. (1995). *Risk*. London: University College of London Press.

Adler, R. and D. Pittle (1984). 'Cajolery and Command: Are Education Campaigns an Adequate Substitute for Regulation?' *Yale Journal on Regulation* 2: 159–194.

Allen, Frederick (1987). 'Unfinished Business: A Comparative Assessment of Environmental Problems'. Washington: US EPA.

Ames, B. N., R. Magaw, and L. S. Gold (1987). 'Ranking Possible Carcinogenic Hazards'. *Science* 236: 271.

Anand, Paul (1991). 'The Nature of Rational Choice and the *Foundations of Statistics*'. *Oxford Economic Papers* 43: 199–216.

—— and Chris Forshner (1995). 'Of Mad Cows and Marmosets: From Rational Choice to Organizational Behavior in Crisis Management'. *British Journal of Management* 6: 221–233.

Arnould, Richard J. and Len M. Nichols (1983). 'Wage–Risk Premiums and Workers' Compensation: A Refinement of Estimates of Compensating Wage Differentials'. *Journal of Political Economy* 91(2): 332–340.

Atkinson, S. E. and R. Halvorsen (1990). 'The Valuation of Risks to Life: Evidence from the Market for Automobiles'. *Review of Economics and Statistics* 72(1): 133–136.

Blomquist, Glenn C. (1988). *The Regulation of Motor Vehicle and Traffic Safety*. Boston: Kluwer Academic Publishers.

—— (1991). 'Motorist Use of Safety Equipment: Expected Benefits or Risk Incompetence'. *Journal of Risk and Uncertainty* 4(2): 135–152.

Breyer, Stephen (1993). *Breaking the Vicious Circle: Toward Effective Risk Regulation*. Cambridge, Mass.: Harvard University Press.

Broder, Ivy (1990). 'The Cost of Accidental Death: A Capital Market Approach'. *Journal of Risk and Uncertainty* 3 (1): 51–64.

Brown, Charles (1980). 'Equalizing Differences in the Labor Market'. *Quarterly Journal of Economics* 94(1): 113–134.

Butler, Richard J. (1983). 'Wage and Injury Rate Responses to Shifting Levels of Workers' Compensation'. In John D. Worrall (ed.), *Safety and the Work Force*. Ithaca, NY: ILR Press, pp. 61–86.

Cahill, Captain Richard A. (1990). *Disasters At Sea: Titanic to Exxon Valdez*. Kings Point, NY: American Merchant Marine Foundation and Nautical Books.

Camerer, Colin F. and Martin Weber (1992). 'Recent Developments in Modeling Preferences: Uncertainty and Ambiguity'. *Journal of Risk and Uncertainty* 5: 325–370.

Cousineau, Jean-Michel, Robert Lacroix, and Anne-Marie Girard (1988). 'Occupational Hazard and Wage Compensating Differentials'. University of Montreal Working Paper.

Crandall, Robert W., Howard K. Gruenspecht, Theodore E. Keeler, and Lester B. Lave (1986). *Regulating the Automobile*. Washington: Brookings Institute.

Cropper, Maureen L., Soma K. Aydede, and Paul R. Portney (1994). 'Preferences for Life Saving Programs: How the Public Discounts Time and Age'. *Journal of Risk and Uncertainty* 8(3): 243–266.

Dillingham, Alan (1985). 'The Influence of Risk Variable Definition on Value-of-Life Estimates'. *Economic Inquiry* 23 (2): 277–294.

Dreyfus, Mark and W. Kip Viscusi (1995). 'Rates of Time Preference and Consumer Valuations of Automobile Safety and Fuel Efficiency'. *Journal of Law and Economics* 38(1): 71–105.

Ellsberg, Daniel (1961). 'Risk, Ambiguity, and the Savage Axioms'. *Quarterly Journal of Economics* 75: 643–669.

Fischhoff, Baruch *et al.* (1981). *Acceptable Risk*. Cambridge: Cambridge University Press.

Gaba, Anil and W. Kip Viscusi (1997). 'Differences in Subjective Risk Thresholds: Worker Groups as an Example'. *Management Science*, forthcoming.

Garen, John E. (1988). 'Compensating Wage Differentials and the Endogeneity of Job Riskiness'. *Review of Economics and Statistics* 70(1): 9–16.

Gately, Dermot (1980). 'Individual Discount Rates and the Purchase and Utilization of Energy-Using Durables: Comment'. *Bell Journal of Economics* 11: 373–374.

Gerking, Shelley, Menno de Haan, and William Schulze (1988). 'The Marginal Value of Job Safety: A Contingent Valuation Approach'. *Journal of Risk and Uncertainty* 1(2): 185–200.

Gold, Lois Swirsky, Thomas U. Sloane, Bonnie R. Stern, Neela B. Manley, and Bruce N. Ames (1992). 'Rodent Carcinogens: Setting Priorities'. *Science* 258: 261–265.

Graham, John D. (1989). *Auto Safety: Assessing America's Performance*. Dover, Mass.: Auburn House Publishing.

—— and Jonathan Wiener (eds.) (1995). *Risk Versus Risk*. Cambridge, Mass.: Harvard University Press.

Hausman, Jerry A. (1979). 'Individual Discount Rates and the Purchase and Utilization of Energy-Using Durables'. *Bell Journal of Economics* 10: 33–54.

Hersch, Joni and W. Kip Viscusi (1990). 'Cigarette Smoking, Seatbelt Use, and Differences in Wage–Risk Tradeoffs'. *Journal of Human Resources* 25: 202–227.

—— and Todd S. Pickton (1995). 'Risk-Taking Activities and Heterogeneity of Job–Risk Tradeoffs'. *Journal of Risk and Uncertainty* 11(3): 205–218.

Herzog, Henry W. Jr and Alan M. Schlottmann (1990). 'Valuing Risk in the Workplace: Market Price, Willingness to Pay, and the Optimal Provision of Safety'. *Review of Economics and Statistics* 72(3): 463–470.

Hopkins, Thomas (1992). 'Costs of Regulation: Filling the Gaps'. Report prepared for the Regulatory Information Service Center, August 1992.

Johnanneson, Magnus and Per Olov Johansson (1996). 'To Be or Not to Be, That Is the Question: An Empirical Study of the WTP for an Increased Life Expectancy at an Advanced Age'. *Journal of Risk and Uncertainty* 13: 163–174.

Jones-Lee, Michael (1974). 'The Value of Changes in the Probability of Death or Injury'. *Journal of Political Economy* 82(4): 835–849.

—— (1989). *The Economics of Safety and Physical Risk*. Oxford: Blackwell.

—— (1991). 'Altruism and the Value of Other People's Safety'. *Journal of Risk and Uncertainty* 4 (2): 213–219.

—— and Graham Loomes (1995). 'Scale and Context Effects in the Valuation of Transport Safety'. *Journal of Risk and Uncertainty* 11(3): 183–204.

Kahneman, Daniel and Amos Tversky (1979). 'Prospect Theory: An Analysis of Decision under Risk'. *Econometrica* 47: 263–291.

Kniesner, Thomas J. and John D. Leeth (1991). 'Compensating Wage Differentials for Fatal Injury Risk in Australia, Japan, and the United States'. *Journal of Risk and Uncertainty* 4(1): 75–90.

—— —— (1995). *Simulating Workplace Safety Policy*. Norwell, Mass.: Kluwer Academic Publishers.

Krier, James (1990). 'Risk and Design'. *Journal of Legal Studies* 19: 781–790.

Kunreuther, H. *et al.* (1978). *Disaster Insurance Protection: Public Policy Lessons*. New York: John Wiley.

Lave, Lester B. (1981). *The Strategy of Social Regulation: Decision Frameworks for Policy*. Washington: Brookings Institute.

Leigh, J. Paul (1987). 'Gender, Firm Size, Industry and Estimates of the Value-of-Life'. *Journal of Health Economics* 6(3): 255–273.

—— and Roger N. Folsom (1984). 'Estimates of the Value of Accident Avoidance at the Job Depend on the Concavity of the Equalizing Differences Curve'. *Quarterly Review of Economics and Business* 24(1): 56–66.

Lichtenstein, S. *et al.* (1978). 'Judged Frequency of Lethal Events'. *Journal of Experimental Psychology* 4: 551–578.

Lutter, Randall and John Morrall (1994). 'Health–Health Analysis: A New Way to Evaluate Health and Safety Regulation'. *Journal of Risk and Uncertainty* 8(1): 43–66.

—— —— and W. Kip Viscusi (1996). 'Risky Behavior and the Income–Mortality Relationship'. Working Paper.

Magat, Wesley A. and W. Kip Viscusi (1992). *Informational Approaches to Regulation*. Cambridge, Mass.: MIT Press.

Marin, Alan and George Psacharopoulos (1982). 'The Reward for Risk in the Labor Market: Evidence from the United Kingdom and a Reconciliation with Other Studies'. *Journal of Political Economy* 90(4): 827–853.

Moore, Michael J. and W. Kip Viscusi (1988*a*). 'Doubling the Estimated Value of Life: Results Using New Occupational Fatality Data'. *Journal of Policy Analysis and Management* 7(3): 476–490.

——— (1988*b*). 'The Quantity-Adjusted Value of Life'. *Economic Inquiry* 26(3): 369–388.

——— (1990*a*). *Compensating Mechanisms for Job Risks: Wages, Workers' Compensation, and Product Liability*. Princeton: Princeton University Press.

——— (1990*b*). 'Models for Estimating Discount Rates for Long-Term Health Risks using Labor Market Data'. *Journal of Risk and Uncertainty* 3(4): 381–402.

Morrall, John F. III (1981). 'A Review of the Record'. *Regulation* 10(2): 13–24, 30–34.

National Safety Council (1994). *Accident Facts*. Itasca, Ill.: National Safety Council.

Nichols, Albert and Richard J. Zeckhauser (1986). 'The Perils of Prudence: How Conservative Risk Assessments Distort Regulation'. *Regulation* 10(2): 13–24.

Noll, Roger and James Krier (1990). 'Some Implications of Cognitive Psychology for Risk Regulation'. *The Journal of Legal Studies* 19: 747–79.

Olson, Craig A. (1981). 'An Analysis of Wage Differentials Received by Workers on Dangerous Jobs'. *Journal of Human Resources* 16(2): 167–185.

Peltzman, S. (1975). 'The Effects of Automobile Safety Regulation'. *Journal of Political Economy* 83(4): 677–725.

Rheingold, P. D. (1990). 'Appendix E'. American Bar Association Commission on Mass Torts, *Report to the House Delegates*, Washington.

Schelling, Thomas (1968). 'The Life You Save May Be Your Own'. In S. Chase (ed.), *Problems in Public Expenditure Analysis*. Washington: Brookings Institute, pp. 127–162.

Sinfield, Nick (1994). 'Asbestos—Human or Natural Disaster?' Paper presented at the Stanford University Conference on Social Treatment of Catastrophic Risk.

Smith, Robert S. (1974). 'The Feasibility of an "Injury Tax" Approach to Occupational Safety'. *Law and Contemporary Problems* 38(4): 730–744.

—— (1976). *The Occupational Safety and Health Act: Its Goals and Achievements*. Washington: American Enterprise Institute.

Smith, V. Kerry and Carol Gilbert (1984). 'The Implicit Risks to Life: A Comparative Analysis'. *Economics Letters* 16: 393–399.

Thaler, R. and S. Rosen (1976). 'The Value of Saving a Life: Evidence from the Labor Market'. In N. Terleckyz (ed.), *Household Production and Consumption*. New York: Columbia University Press, pp. 265–298.

Tobacco Institute (1991). *The Tax Burden on Tobacco*, Washington: Tobacco Institute.

—— (1996). *The Tax Burden on Tobacco*. Washington: Tobacco Institute.

Viscusi, W. Kip (1978a). 'Labor Market Valuations of Life and Limb: Empirical Estimates and Policy Implications'. *Public Policy* 26(3): 359–386.

—— (1978b). 'Wealth Effects and Earnings Premiums for Job Hazards'. *Review of Economics and Statistics* 60(3): 408–416.

—— (1979). *Employment Hazards: An Investigation of Market Performance*. Cambridge, Mass.: Harvard University Press.

—— (1981). 'Occupational Safety and Health Regulation: Its Impact and Policy Alternatives'. In J. Crecine (ed.), *Research in Public Policy Analysis and Management*, vol. 2. Greenwich, Conn.: JAI Press, pp. 281–299.

—— (1983). *Risk by Choice: Regulating Health and Safety in the Workplace*. Cambridge, Mass.: Harvard University Press.

—— (1985). 'Consumer Behavior and the Safety Effects of Product Safety Regulation'. *Journal of Law and Economics* 28: 527–554.

—— (1990a). 'Do Smokers Underestimate Risks?' *Journal of Political Economy* 98(6): 1253–1269.

—— (1990b). 'Sources of Inconsistency in Societal Responses to Health Risks'. *American Economic Review* 80(2): 257–261.

—— (1991). *Reforming Products Liability*. Cambridge, Mass.: Harvard University Press.

—— (1992a). *Fatal Tradeoffs: Public and Private Responsibilities for Risk*. New York: Oxford University Press.

—— (1992b). *Smoking: Making the Risky Decision*. New York: Oxford University Press.

—— (1993). 'The Risky Business of Insurance Pricing'. *Journal of Risk and Uncertainty* 7(1): 117–139.

—— (1994a). 'Mortality Effects of Regulatory Costs and Policy Evaluation Criteria'. *Rand Journal of Economics* 25(1): 94–109.

—— (1994b). 'Risk–Risk Analysis'. *Journal of Risk and Uncertainty* 8(1): 5–17.

—— (1995). 'Cigarette Taxation and the Social Consequences of Smoking'. In James Poterba (ed.), *Tax Policy and the Economy*, vol. 9. National Bureau of Economic Research, pp. 51–101.

—— (1997). 'Alarmist Decisions with Divergent Risk Information'. *Economic Journal* 107: 445.

—— and Gerald Cavallo (1994). 'The Effect of Product Safety Regulation on Safety Precautions'. *Risk Analysis* 15(6): 917–930.

—— and Harell Chesson (1997). 'Hopes and Fears: The Conflicting Effects of Risk Ambiguity'. Working Paper.

Viscusi, W. Kip and W. Evans (1990). 'Utility Functions that Depend on Health Status: Estimates and Economic Implications'. *American Economic Review* 80(2): 353–374.

Viscusi, W. Kip and Jahn K. Hakes (1997). 'Synthetic Risks, Risk Potency, and Carcinogen Regulation'. *Journal of Policy Analysis and Management*, forthcoming.

—— and James T. Hamilton (1996). 'Are Risk Regulators Rational? Evidence from Hazardous Waste Cleanup Decisions'. Working Paper.

—— and Joni Hersch (1990). 'The Market Response to Product Safety Litigation'. *Journal of Regulatory Economics* 2(3): 213–230.

—— and Wesley A. Magat (1987). *Learning about Risk: Consumer and Worker Responses to Hazard Information*. Cambridge, Mass.: Harvard University Press.

———— and Joel Huber (1987). 'An Investigation of the Rationality of Consumer Valuations of Multiple Health Risks'. *Rand Journal of Economics* 18(4): 465–479.

———— (1991). 'Communication of Ambiguous Risk Information'. *Theory and Decision* 31(2/3): 159–173.

—— and Michael J. Moore (1987). 'Workers' Compensation: Wage Effects, Benefit Inadequacies, and the Value of Health Losses'. *Review of Economics and Statistics* 69: 249–261.

———— (1989). 'Rates of Time Preference and Valuations of the Duration of Life'. *Journal of Public Economics* 38: 297–317.

—— and Charles O'Connor (1984). 'Adaptive Responses to Chemical Labeling: Are Workers Bayesian Decision Makers?' *American Economic Review* 74(5): 942–956.

—— John M. Vernon, and Joseph Harrington, Jr (1995). *Economics of Regulation and Antitrust*. Cambridge, Mass.: MIT Press.

—— and Richard J. Zeckhauser (1994). 'The Fatality and Injury Costs of Expenditures'. *Journal of Risk and Uncertainty* 8(1): 271–293. Reprinted in W. Kip Viscusi (ed.), *The Mortality Costs of Regulatory Expenditures*. Boston: Kluwer Academic Publishers, 1995.

Wagenaar, William A. (1992). 'Risk Taking and Accident Causation'. In J. Frank Yates (ed.), *Risk-Taking Behavior*. Chichester, Sussex: John Wiley.

Weiler, Paul (1991). *Medical Malpractice on Trial*. Cambridge, Mass.: Harvard University Press.

Wilson, Richard (1979). 'Analyzing the Daily Risks of Life'. *Technology Review* 81(4): 40–46.

Yates, J. Frank (ed.) (1992). *Risk-Taking Behavior*. Chichester, Sussex: John Wiley.

Zeckhauser, Richard J. (1975). 'Procedures for Valuing Lives'. *Public Policy* 23(4): 419–464.

—— and Donald Shepard (1976). 'Where Now for Saving Lives'. *Law and Contemporary Problems* 39: 5–45.

Index